© THE BAKER & TAYLOR CO.

ANDROPOV

ANDROPOV

Zhores Medvedev

W. W. Norton and Company
New York · London

© Zhores A. Medvedev 1983

First American Edition 1983

ISBN 0-393-01791-5

Printed in Great Britain

Contents

Preface

This book considers recent developments in the Soviet Union but is based on materials which I have been accumulating for several years. When Brezhnev began to display obvious signs of physical decline in 1975 discussion began, openly in the West and surreptitiously in the Soviet Union, about the question of succession. The problem of achieving an orderly change of leader by established procedures has not yet been solved in the Soviet Union or in any of the other Communist countries. With the exception of Khrushchev, Soviet leaders have died while in office. Without exception their poorest performances and most painful errors have been made towards the end of their natural or political lives. This is true even of Lenin – he knew that it was wrong to appoint Stalin General Secretary of the Party in 1922. But by the time he wanted to remove Stalin from this position, he was no longer able to ensure that his recommendations were accepted. He left a political testament requesting that Stalin be replaced, but his wishes were ignored.

Stalin's tyranny lasted throughout his long tenure of office, but his paranoia increased during the last few years of his life. It was then that he launched a new wave of terror at home and embarked upon dangerous adventures abroad such as the Berlin blockade and the Korean war. Khrushchev was removed in a palace coup because his political and economic measures of 1962–64 threatened to create a crisis. It is true of Brezhnev, too, that his last years in office were his most unsuccessful. Economic growth was slowing down, agricultural production had declined, and the international position of the USSR was under heavy criticism from all sides because of the invasion of Afghanistan and events in Poland. Relations with the West deteriorated and the policy of détente seemed to be changing rapidly into a new Cold War. Brezhnev was not entirely responsible for all these developments, but his poor health made him unable to react to new challenges in an energetic or effective manner.

Changes in the leadership of the Soviet Union are so rare that they are treated like revolutions. Brezhnev was in office for eighteen years. During that time he dealt with five American Presidents and four British Prime Ministers. This long tenure of office makes the position of Soviet leader the most powerful in the world. The United States may be the most powerful nation in an economic and military sense, but American Presidents can only initiate particular programmes – they are unlikely to be in office long enough to see a programme through from beginning to end. Soviet leaders are not bound by such restrictions of time, nor are they hampered like American Presidents by Congress or by public opinion. It is this enormous power which makes a change in Soviet leadership an event of international importance.

The change finally took place on 10 November 1982, after Brezhnev's death. The death itself came as no surprise, but it had not been expected that the man elected to succeed as General Secretary of the Communist Party of the Soviet Union would be Yuri Vladimirovich Andropov, the former head of the KGB, a man who was certainly not Brezhnev's choice. The fact that he was not Brezhnev's choice became increasingly apparent in the last few years. In this book I will attempt to explain how this succession came about and to draw some conclusions about what the world can expect from the new Soviet leadership.

I would like to thank my brother Roy, whose books on Stalin and Khrushchev and essays on Brezhnev's period in office have helped to inform my political analysis. Roy has also corrected some of my judgements about the events of recent months. He would certainly help me much more if we were able to communicate in ways other than via censored correspondence between London and Moscow and difficult telephone conversations which are listened to and recorded by the Soviet authorities.

For a former Soviet citizen and dissident, writing about the previous head of the KGB is not an easy task. I have endeavoured to make this book as scholarly as possible and to write without personal emotions. But I have had the same problem (possibly purely psychological) as other writers, whatever their nationality, who have written about security services – a reluctance to reveal the subject matter of my research before the manuscript is safely at the publishers. For this reason I have taken less advice from friends and colleagues than I would have liked. To those friends who have read the manuscript and helped me to improve the English I am very grateful.

Zhores A. Medvedev
London

Part One

The Power Struggle in the Kremlin

1

The Beginning of the Power Struggle

For Stalin, Khrushchev and Brezhnev the real power struggle started after they had been elected to the top position in the Communist Party. Yuri Andropov's struggle for power began long before his elevation to the position of General Secretary.

Speculation about a succession problem in the Kremlin began in 1975, when Brezhnev suffered a stroke and disappeared from active political life for several months. During his long period of recuperation Mikhail Suslov and Andrei Kirilenko shared the Party leadership, Alexei Kosygin was in full control of the government, while Nikolai Podgorny was in charge of the Presidium of the Supreme Soviet. They were all men of around seventy, but if Brezhnev should die they were in a position to form a new collective leadership. The most responsible position was, of course, that of General Secretary. Suslov, who was already seventy-three, was too old to initiate a new era and the main problem would be to organize a reasonable succession through the Secretariat.

The Secretariat is the group of ten secretaries of the Party Central Committee which runs Party and state affairs on a day-to-day basis and makes many important appointments. For a fuller explanation of the Soviet political system, readers are referred to the Appendix. The General Secretary is, in fact, a position which was created in 1922 for the Secretariat, and not for the Politburo as is often suggested in the West. In 1922 there was a separate Chairman of the Politburo, a position which was later abolished. Regional Party committees also have secretariats, and the seniority of various secretaries is clearly indicated since they are called First, Second and Third Secretary. The Central Committee Secretariat also contains a hierarchy, but the ranks of seniority are not expressed in official titles. The Second Secretary is in charge of the Secretariat when the General Secretary is on holiday, ill, abroad, or away from Moscow for any reason. Before 1976 Andrei Kirilenko acted as Second Secretary, and Mikhail Suslov acted in this capacity for the five or six years before his death.

After 1964, when Suslov and Alexander Shelepin successfully organized Khrushchev's dismissal, Suslov was considered to be Brezhnev's rival and possible successor in the case of a leadership crisis. But when Shelepin was discharged from the Politburo in 1975, Suslov became a lonely figure who presented no threat to Brezhnev. As the longest-serving member of the Central Committee (he had been elected to the Central Revision Commission at the Eighteenth Party Congress in 1939 and was promoted to membership of the Central Committee in 1941), he was the natural choice for the number two position in the Secretariat. Each secretary of the Central Committee has a clearly defined 'sphere of influence'. Mikhail Gorbachev, for example, is currently the secretary for agriculture and Vladimir Dolgikh secretary for industry. Konstantin Rusakov supervises links with Communist Parties in socialist countries, while Boris Ponamarev does the same for Communist Parties in the capitalist world. In general terms Suslov was the secretary for ideology, or Chief Ideologue. In practice this meant that he supervised very many fields and was at the top of a large pyramid which included the Central Committee departments of propaganda, culture, science and education and both international departments. He also controlled the Political Directorate of the Army and Navy, the Komsomol, the media and the State Committee for Publishing, the Committee for Cinema, censorship, TASS and Novosty

Press, the Ministry of Culture, Radio and Television, the Writers' Union and the other 'creative' unions (composers, artists, journalists, etc.), all 'friendship' societies with other countries, the All-Union Peace Committee, the Academy of Sciences, primary, secondary and higher education systems, and the relations of the state with various religions and with the churches, as well as a number of other organizations. No important appointments in these numerous fields were possible without Suslov's approval.

When Brezhnev returned after his long absence he showed clear signs of continuing ill health and was no longer able to work as hard as before. Nonetheless he still tried to consolidate his position as leader. In 1977 he unexpectedly assumed the office of Chairman of the Presidium of the Supreme Soviet. The previous incumbent, his old colleague Nikolai Podgorny, was offered the position of Deputy Chairman to replace V. V. Kuznetsov, who was seventy-six in 1977. But Podgorny strongly objected to Brezhnev's appointment and was, therefore, simply sent into retirement. Moreover, Brezhnev began to use the office of President, previously a nominal and ceremonial role, as a means of promoting his own influence. As he became older, Brezhnev, who had been rather a modest man, became jealous of his place in history. He wanted to make arrangements in the leadership which would guarantee that the internal and foreign policies identified with his name would continue after his death. After the Twenty-Fifth Party Congress in 1976 he had decided to increase the size of the Politburo from eleven to fourteen members in order to appoint some of his close friends. Konstantin Chernenko, who had been his personal assistant, was promoted to candidate member of the Politburo, and many other personal aides and assistants became members and candidate members of the Central Committee.

In 1978 Brezhnev's health deteriorated further, and speculation in the foreign press about the Kremlin succession started in earnest. Many suggestions were made about the possible successor, though there were no clear indications about who it would be. Even Edmund Stevens, the longest-serving British journalist in Moscow (he was present, as the *Manchester Guardian* correspondent, at the show trials in 1937 and 1938), who heard all the rumours in the Party apparatus and who started speculating about Brezhnev's successor at the very beginning of 1978, could not be specific. There were no signs yet of Brezhnev's own preference (Chernenko was still only a candidate member of the Politburo), and Stevens came to the simplest conclusion that 'logic would suggest one of the younger members of the Politburo'. In 1978 this indicated Grigorii Romanov.

> Romanov joined the Politburo in 1976, and it was then thought he was being groomed for the succession. He is good-looking, urbane, well-educated, an eloquent speaker and has an impressive war record. Moreover, as party chief in Leningrad – the old imperial capital, now known as the cradle of the revolution – he occupies one of the most eminent posts in the hierarchy.[1]

When Chernenko was promoted to full membership of the Politburo in 1979, this was taken as a clear sign of Brezhnev's own preference. Victor Zorza, another very experienced 'Kremlin watcher', was convinced that Chernenko was 'a faithful aide who is being groomed for leadership'.[2]

I was of a quite different opinion at this time. In an article published in 1979 I expressed my views about the main contenders for power as follows:

> If Brezhnev himself decided to retire and pick his successor, then Chernenko might be installed as the new leader. But while he is close to Brezhnev as a colleague, Chernenko is absolutely unknown to the country and in the party as a whole: he is a typical apparatchik without credentials, practical authority or a power base (he is part of Brezhnev's power base). Hence I do not expect much support for him. To pinpoint the most likely choice for General Secretary is

very difficult now, but I suspect that Andropov, who was responsible for foreign affairs in the Secretariat before he was put in charge of security, has more chance of getting the post: he has accumulated real power in the last few years.[3]

My brother, Roy Medvedev, who lives in Moscow, shared this view and often expressed it in private conversations with journalists.

After Suslov's death in January 1982 Kremlin watchers tried hard to detect any minor (often insignificant) indication of Brezhnev's likely successor. The method favoured by Kremlinologists is to analyse the way in which the leading figures perform at official functions. At the beginning of March, *Time* magazine reported that

As Kremlinologists scrutinized the line-up of Politburo members waiting to greet Poland's General Wojciech Jaruzelski, they noticed a subtle, but possibly important, change. Konstantin Chernenko, 70, a burly, longtime crony of Soviet President Leonid Brezhnev's, occupied the No. 3 position in the receiving line. Only Premier Nikolai Tikhonov, whose presence was required by protocol, stood closer to the ailing Soviet leader. The white-maned Chernenko's commanding position set off speculation that he had won a round or two in the behind-the-scenes struggle to succeed the 75-year-old Brezhnev.

The article went on:

But whether Kirilenko or Chernenko wins out, either one of the septuagenarians could end up serving only as a caretaker while such 'younger' Politburo members as Viktor Grishin, 67, and Grigori Romanov, 59, vie for position.[4]

Other Moscow correspondents made different predictions. Those who based their judgements on official briefings were usually in favour of Chernenko. However, a few more investigative reporters were describing a much more complex power struggle. In fact, Suslov's position in the Secretariat was contested almost immediately and there was a strong rumour in Moscow that Andropov would get this job. It was also known that Brezhnev favoured Chernenko. Kirilenko no longer played an active role in Central Committee affairs since he suffered from progressive arteriosclerosis. There were several political changes at lower levels of the hierarchy in March, mostly to replace Suslov's men in the social science sector of the Academy, in the media and the Trade Unions. The dismissal of Alexei Shibaev on 5 March from the Chairmanship of the Trade Union Council was not related to the events in Poland, as was suspected, but was the beginning of general personnel changes in the Kremlin. Shibaev was Suslov's protégé and a loyal Brezhnev supporter, but he was an inexperienced and ineffectual trade-unionist and there was pressure for his removal from below as well as from the top.

From 1977 onwards Brezhnev's doctors had prescribed two holidays for him each year, the first in March, a difficult time for elderly people with a heart condition. He used to spend every March in his residence at Sochi in the Krasnodar region and would return to Moscow in April when the weather in Central Russia had improved. He preferred his Crimean residence for his summer holiday, and it was here that he used to meet Eastern European leaders. However, Suslov's death changed the normal routine. It was not clear who would stay in Moscow in charge of Suslov's vast ideological and political apparatus. Ustinov, Shcherbitsky and some other Politburo members wanted to promote Andropov; however, Brezhnev and Tikhonov were insistent in their support for Chernenko. In these circumstances, Brezhnev's traditional departure for a spring holiday could influence the situation, and his supporters decided that it would be better for him to stay in Moscow to preside over the Politburo and over state affairs in general. As an excuse for cancelling his holiday, Brezhnev decided that he would personally deliver the Order of Lenin, awarded for achievements in the development of agriculture and industry, to the Uzbek Republic. In fact, in 1982, the sixtieth anniversary of the formation of the Union of Soviet Socialist Republics, every republic was awarded as Order of Lenin. Although Brezhnev was Chairman of the Supreme Soviet he was not, of course, expected to deliver all these awards personally, so it was clearly merely an excuse for going to Tashkent. It was also intended that the trip should demonstrate how fit Brezhnev was: he was to make an important speech in Tashkent containing a new overture to China. There were even rumours that he would have a secret meeting there with a high Chinese official – an unlikely event since diplomatic protocol would have required him to meet the Chinese head of state, and even secret negotiations would have involved many aides and experts. Therefore these rumours also seem to have been a way of justifying an unexpected trip.

This trip, from which so much was expected, turned into a disaster for Brezhnev's supporters. His departure from Tashkent was given nationwide coverage, and television crews were waiting for him to arrive back in Moscow. Shortly before the plane landed Brezhnev suffered a mild stroke. The crowd which had been assembled at the airport was asked to disperse. When the plane landed an unconscious Brezhnev was taken on a stretcher to the specially equipped car which appeared identical to his official car but was fitted out for medical emergencies. (For some years these two cars had always stood by in case of need.) He was taken to a special section of the Kremlin hospital in a state of coma and remained unconscious for several days, in a critical condition. Inevitably, there were rumours that he had died. In fact he recovered, but lost the power of speech for several weeks. The April Central Committee Plenum was postponed indefinitely. It was during this illness that Andropov managed to consolidate his position.

Rumours about the succession became even stronger during Brezhnev's April illness. Chernenko still seemed the most obvious choice to many foreign journalists. *Time* magazine maintained that

The most visible contender at the moment appears to be

Brezhnev Aide Konstantin Chernenko, 70, who is now seen in official photographs standing beside Brezhnev. According to some reports, Chernenko is in charge of the Kremlin's day-to-day affairs. Other Politburo members vying for the succession include Moscow Party Boss Viktor Grishin, Leningrad Party Boss Grigori Romanov and KGB Chief Yuri Andropov.[5]

While *Newsweek*'s experts on Soviet affairs also put Konstantin Chernenko as first choice, they thought it possible that

. . . power may pass directly to a younger generation of Kremlin leaders; in that case, Mikhail Gorbachev, 51, the promising party secretary for agriculture, seems to be the front runner. But for the immediate post-Brezhnev period at least, the odds still run heavily in favor of a caretaker government led by men of Brezhnev's generation.[6]

However, Lenin's birthday celebrations at the end of April gave a better indication of who was really in command. Andropov had already begun to act as head of Suslov's ideological empire during Brezhnev's absence and it was he who was chosen to make the traditional speech marking Lenin's brithday on 22 April. Brezhnev made an appearance at this meeting, ending the rumours that he was already totally incapacitated. Although Andropov was still the nominal head of the KGB, he now preferred to spend most of his working day in the Central Committee office which is almost opposite the well-known KGB building on Dzerzhinsky Square. Some Moscow sources were reporting that the most likely new head of the KGB was Geidar Aliyev, candidate Politburo member from Azerbaijan, who had been a professional KGB officer before 1969.

The Central Committee meeting which had been postponed because of Brezhnev's illness finally took place in late May. It was no secret to Brezhnev's close colleagues that he had been in a state of 'clinical death' for a few minutes after his stroke and had only been revived by the resuscitation equipment. He was expected to leave Moscow to convalesce in the Crimea after the Plenum. The main task confronting the Plenum was the election of a new 'Chief Ideologue', and this election became, in effect, a rehearsal for the election of Brezhnev's successor.

Chernenko's only qualification for the position was Brezhnev's support. He was Brezhnev's chief aide and the manager of his personal office. However, he had become a full member of the Politburo much later than the other members, and even Brezhnev's close friends Dinmukhamed Kunaev and Vladimir Shcherbitsky objected to working under someone whom they regarded as their junior. Gorbachev, Gromyko and Ustinov were also against Chernenko's appointment. Although they were all loyal to Brezhnev, their loyalty did not extend to his protégés, and Brezhnev himself was not strong enough to press a suggestion which was clearly not based on merit. The only candidate who was well qualified for Suslov's job was Yuri Andropov. He had worked under Suslov's supervision from 1957 to 1967 as head of the foreign (socialist) department of the Central Committee before he became a Politburo member. In October 1956 Khrushchev had sent Suslov to Hungary to supervise developments there, and as Soviet Ambassador to Hungary Andropov had worked under Suslov's direct command for two months. It was Suslov who recommended Andropov for the post of head of the Central Committee foreign department in 1957. When Andropov became Chairman of the KGB, part of the staff of the Ideological Commission of the Central Committee was transferred to the KGB, which began to play a more important role in the ideological sphere. A number of agencies responsible for censorship and postal surveillance, etc., as well as academic institutes such as the Institute of the United States of Canada and the Institute of the Far East, were put under a complex system of controls coming from Suslov's apparatus, from the KGB and from the Academy of

Sciences of the USSR. There were no other suitable candidates for Suslov's position amongst the Politburo members. Andrei Kirilenko, at seventy-five, was already too old, and ill. Younger men like Viktor Grishin and Grigorii Romanov, Party leaders of Moscow and Leningrad respectively, were notorious for their opulent and corrupt life-styles – they were clearly ill-suited to give ideological instruction to others. It was unlikely that a non-Russian member of the Politburo would be chosen. Andropov, therefore, had no serious rivals for the second place in the Party hierarchy.

Nonetheless the Politburo meeting at which the decision was taken was rather heated and the discussion lasted six hours. Brezhnev had no really valid objections to Andropov's election. Until the end of 1981 he had enjoyed good relations with him. The reasons for their estrangement (which I discuss later) could hardly be used by him to instigate a blocking move.

Once Andropov had been elevated to the Secretariat it became necessary to appoint a new Chairman of the KGB. Brezhnev favoured Geidar Aliyev for this position, but once again his proposal did not receive the necessary support. Andropov was entitled to recommend his successor, and he suggested Vitalii Fedorchuk, the little-known head of the KGB in the Ukraine, a proposal supported by Shcherbitsky, First Secretary of the Ukrainian Central Committee. Fedorchuk was a professional military man who had distinguished himself by suppressing nationalism in his native republic. He could be relied upon to play a non-political role, whereas Aliyev, a long-standing candidate member of the Politburo, was due to be promoted to full membership, particularly since he had a good record as Party boss of Azerbaijan. The other appointments made at the May Plenum were less controversial. Vladimir Dolgikh, aged fifty-seven, was elected as a candidate member of the Politburo, a move widely regarded as an indication of his possible future promotion to the post of Chairman of the Council of Ministers. Nikolai Tikhonov, Brezhnev's friend since the 1930s, who had been appointed Premier shortly before Alexei Kosygin's death at the end of 1980, was, at seventy-seven, already old and weak. Brezhnev managed to promote one of his own men too: Professor Evgenii Chazov, a prominent cardiologist and the chief doctor of the Kremlin hospital, and the 'guardian' of Brezhnev's heart, was promoted to full membership of the Central Committee. He had been a candidate member since the Twenty-Sixth Party Congress.

For Soviet citizens Andropov's promotion from the KGB to Suslov's post in the Party Secretariat was an unmistakable sign. He had moved from the sixth position in the Party hierarchy to the second. Foreign journalists reporting from Moscow found to their great surprise that Muscovites were looking forward to having a new leader, despite Andropov's KGB background. Russians were not only ready for change, they also wanted a strong man at their head. For some time foreign visitors had been amazed by an apparent revival in Stalin's popularity. Pictures of Stalin reappeared in private apartments and publicly in the windows of taxi-cabs. In Georgia, where he had never lost his popularity, photographs of Stalin could be brought for as little as a rouble on the 'black market', and from there they were exported to other parts of the country. This was a silent demonstration against Brezhnev's inefficient rule and artificial 'personality cult'. A *Newsweek* correspondent, Andrew Nagorsky, was one of the few foreign correspondents who could speak perfect Russian. He was also an investigative journalist, and he set out to get the opinion not only of officials but also of people from other walks of life. In June 1982 he reported:

> Russians ranging from embattled dissidents to stodgy apparatchiks have been painting Andropov as the liberal-minded reformer. 'Westerners see him only as a person of the KGB', says one well-briefed Soviet official in Moscow. 'But we see him as intelligent, open to new ideas and more progressive than the current leadership.'
>
> That sort of remark – typical in Moscow these days – is

doubly surprising. Two years ago few Russians would dare talk openly about Brezhnev's impending departure within earshot of the KGB. Now it is the talk of the town, and the current favorite, the KGB's Andropov, is described in largely positive terms. Intellectuals say he is more sympathetic to expanding their role in policy formation. Some Jewish dissidents believe he is not as anti-Semitic as other high Soviet officials. And some party insiders say Andropov's total lack of experience in agriculture and industrial planning may prove beneficial given the country's dismal economic performance under Brezhnev. Many Soviets even say that his tenure at the KGB marks him as a closet liberal. 'He did not repeat any of the more brutal repressions of the past', says one social scientist. 'Andropov only did what any KGB chief would have done in his place.'[7]

Nagorsky's informants were, of course, from the educated classes and could discern the differences between Andropov and Chernenko. Ordinary Muscovites and peoples in the provinces knew very little about Andropov, had not heard the rumours that were circulating in Moscow and were apparently apprehensive about him just because of his KGB background. However, they knew even less about Chernenko or other Politburo members.

Unfortunately Nagorsky was new to Moscow. He had not yet realized that no official, whether pro-Andropov or pro-Chernenko, would be tolerant of a foreign correspondent who wanted to carry out a genuine public opinion poll. A few weeks after the publication of this article, Nagorsky was declared *persona non grata* and was ordered to leave Moscow within a few days. The US State Department retaliated by sending home the *Izvestiya* Washington correspondent.

2

Andropov as 'Chief Ideologue', May – November 1982

Soon after the May Plenum Brezhnev left for his summer residence in the Crimea. Andropov was now in charge of the Secretariat and the most influential member of the Politburo. It was unlikely that there would be any important Politburo meetings during the summer. The introduction of the new 'Food Programme' had been delayed until the end of May, and provincial members and candidate members of the Politburo like Kunaev, Aliyev, Shcherbitsky and Eduard Shevarnadze were charged with the urgent task of improving agricultural efficiency. Mikhail Gorbachev, the Central Committee secretary for agriculture, was also touring the country. The weather was bad during the spring of 1982 and there were already signs of drought in the agriculturally important southern regions of the country. This was the fourth bad season in succession. Early in June the US Department of Agriculture forecast that the Soviet harvest would be 170 million tonnes, 70 million short of the annual plan. This was a poor start for Brezhnev's 'Food Programme'. Although the June and July rains improved the situation, the 1982 harvest still fell short of the target.

An important indication of Andropov's confidence during the summer was the dismissal of two regional Party secretaries, E. V. Rusakov of the Kuibyshev region (brother of K. V. Rusakov, a Central Party Committee secretary) and S. F. Medunov of the Krasnodar region, an old personal friend of Brezhnev, on charges of corruption. Both should have been dismissed before this, since investigations made by the KGB and the General Procurator's office had implicated them in illegal activities. In Rusakov's case these were related to irregularities in the sales of Zhiguli and Lada cars built in the main Soviet Fiat car plant in the Kuibyshev region. The charge against Medunov was more complex, and is discussed in greater detail in Chapter 9. Brezhnev had apparently prevented the removal of the two men from their positions, but in his absence Andropov used his new-found prominence to dismiss them and to order the arrest of many lower-ranking officials in both regions.

After his summer convalescence Brezhnev visited Baku, capital of Azerbaijan, in September. An elaborate programme was planned which included a television broadcast of his speech, to demonstrate his recovery. It was during this speech that a bizarre episode occurred which seemed to show the very opposite. A. M. Aleksandrov-Agentov, Brezhnev's aide, gave him the wrong text to read. It was only after seven minutes had passed that the mistake was noticed, and then not by Brezhnev himself. Aleksandrov-Agentov went up to him, stopped him without any apology, put another text in front of him and said: 'From this one.' Brezhnev looked puzzled, then realized what had happened and told the audience: 'It was not my fault. I have to start all over again now.' The rest of his Baku speech was read by an announcer instead of being broadcast live. The next day Brezhnev was ill again and all his other engagements in Azerbaijan were cancelled. An error of this kind was unprecedented, and was inexcusable for an aide, who would certainly expect immediate dismissal as a result. This may well have been Aleksandrov-Agentov's fate after the Baku fiasco. However, in the brief reports about Andropov's meetings with foreign leaders after Brezhnev's funeral in November, Aleksandrov-Agentov's name was mentioned once again, now in the capacity of assistant to the new General Secretary. Brezhnev's other assistants and aides all failed to keep their positions: Aleksandrov-Agentov was the sole survivor.

Since 1977, Andropov had been given credit in the West for a degree of 'liberalism' mainly through articles written by Boris Rabbot, who had emigrated to the United States in 1976. Rabbot had been a Senior Researcher in the Institute of Sociology in Moscow and claimed to be a member of the circle of Brezhnev's aides and speech writers, almost Brezhnev's personal friend. (There is some doubt as to his real position in Brezhnev's circle of aides. However, as a member of the staff of the Institute of Sociology he apparently took part in discussions on Soviet policy and was privy to many of the current rumours.) He maintained that 'Andropov's liberal views would surprise people in the West' and that he proposed allowing private restaurants and beauty parlours – although he considered that 'his future as a leader is hindered by a liver ailment that requires constant treatment'.[1] Suslov had been thought of as dogmatic and suspicious of subversive foreign influences, and as a secretary of the Central Committee from 1957 to 1967 Andropov had appeared more tolerant of Western ideas and more pragmatic as an administrator. However, in August 1982 the direct-dial telephone link between the international network and the Soviet Union, which had been introduced in 1979 as one of the conditions of the 1980 Olympic Games being held in Moscow, was suddenly disconnected. The Soviet international telephone code was cancelled and the number of lines via the operator was not increased to the pre-1979 level. Telephoning Moscow became extremely difficult with long or indefinite delays, and calling other Soviet cities and towns became almost impossible. On 1 September a new restriction was introduced which severely limited the exchange of information. There was a ban on mailing printed materials abroad, irrespective of subject-matter or date of publication. Only official institutional mailing of printed matter was allowed without a permit. Any individual, Soviet or foreign, who wanted to send books abroad had to get a permit from the Commission on Cultural Exchange in the State Libraries and had to pay a customs duty of 100 per cent. Postal restrictions like these had not existed since Stalin's times. The censorship of letters was also increased and many letters, even those which had been registered, began to disappear again. Fewer Soviet citizens were given permission to travel abroad and academic exchange became very difficult.

The KGB also acquired a new image. Although Andropov, as KGB boss, had received the military rank of general, he did not consider himself to be a military man and never wore a military uniform. This became the style for other KGB officers as well. Vitalii Fedorchuk, a professional soldier who had served in the combat units of the KGB which had fought Ukrainian nationalists in the forests of the Western Ukraine from 1944 to 1947, changed this tradition immediately. His first directive concerned the compulsory wearing of KGB military uniform, in order to emphasize the fact that KGB men are professional military personnel. Many KGB officials did not even possess a uniform, yet they now found that they had to have three different ones, for everyday work, for the field, and for parades and jubilees. This 'militarization' of the KGB effectively reduced its political standing.

The struggle between Chernenko's and Andropov's supporters resumed at the beginning of October, when Brezhnev's condition improved after the heart spasm he had suffered in Azerbaijan. It now took the form of petty personal accusations. There were rumours about Andropov's possible non-Russian origin. His mother's maiden name sounds Jewish and it is possible that Andropov is at least one-quarter Jewish. His surname is not a very common Russian one, and because he was born in the North Caucasus some rumours suggested that his original name had been Andropian, i.e. Armenian. His late wife was also said to have been Jewish. Russian nationalism constitutes a very strong undercurrent in some official circles, and these rumours were attempts to discredit Andropov. At the same time Chernenko's supporters firmly maintained that despite his Ukrainian surname he was pure Russian. A myth about Chernenko's liberal attitudes was put into circulation. It was said to be Chernenko who had given permission for the staging of Mikhail Shatrov's controversial play about Lenin, *So We Shall Triumph,* which in part criticizes Stalin as an insolent, brutal leader. All plays, films or books about Lenin have to be approved and censored by either the ideological department of the Central Committee or by the Politburo itself, and this particular play, which had been rehearsed at the beginning of 1981, had been banned by Suslov. When it was eventually performed, it was very popular in Moscow.

By October Andrei Kirilenko was in trouble and his membership of the Politburo was suspended. On the eve of the October Revolution celebrations, when pictures of the leaders are traditionally displayed in Moscow, Kirilenko's picture was absent, giving rise to much speculation amongst Soviet citizens and foreign correspondents. Foreign newspapers published 'unconfirmed reports' about the defection of Kirilenko's son, an official in foreign trade. (These rumours seem to have had some foundation, but, for reasons which are still unclear, his attempt to remain abroad was unsuccessful and he was returned home and arrested by the KGB.) This improved Andropov's position, since Kirilenko belonged to the Brezhnev faction of the Politburo. Although he was not happy about Chernenko's promotion, in the final count he would have voted for him rather than for Andropov.

3

General Secretary of the Central Committee

Leonid Ilich Brezhnev died from a heart attack at 8.30 a.m. on 10 November 1982. As is usual in such cases, the circumstances of his death were not disclosed. Later, however, some information began to filter through. Brezhnev is said to have died during breakfast, after leaving the room to get something from his study. His wife, who remained in the dining-room, began to worry when he did not return after several minutes. She found him lying unconscious on the floor of his study and she immediately raised the alarm. Brezhnev's personal doctors were on duty twenty-four hours a day, and kept resuscitation and first-aid equipment in the room next to his apartment. This equipment had saved his life when he had suffered a stroke in 1975. Then, his condition had been critical for four hours, and Shelepin had begun preliminary consultations about the succession – an act of precipitousness which cost him his Politburo position once Brezhnev recovered. Now the doctors again battled several hours to save him, but this time without success – the few critical minutes lost before the alarm was raised rendered his state of 'clinical death' irreversible. It was only at 12.30 p.m., when a team of doctors had declared him to be dead, that special measures of general 'alert' were activated. The Taman and Kantemir Guard divisions which are always located in the suburbs of Moscow were put on the alert, and all KGB employees and policemen were ordered not to leave their offices or posts at the end of their normal working day. When the second shift arrived the

There is always factions.

number of KGB people and policemen on duty doubled. An enlarged Politburo (members, candidate members, some key Central Committee members and Marshals) met at 4 p.m. This body under the chairmanship of Shcherbitsky, almost immediately elected Andropov as General Secretary. It was Marshal Ustinov who proposed him for the post. Chernenko already knew that Tikhonov, his main supporter, stood no chance of obtaining a majority for him, Aliyev, formerly considered a strong adherent of the Brezhnev faction, had changed sides. Although Aliyev was not yet a full member of the Politburo, his support for Andropov was very important. To avoid any obvious signs of disunity it was promised that Chernenko would be made Chairman of the Presidium of the Supreme Soviet. However, two weeks after Brezhnev's death the situation had changed and the post was left vacant. Chernenko, it was clear, was not welcome in any influential position.

According to the Party Rules, the General Secretary is actually elected by the Plenum of the Central Committee. In Stalin's time this body had merely a rubber-stamp function. Khrushchev, however, had reactivated it, and in 1957 it had saved him from the 'anti-Party Group', which had a majority in the Politburo. (In 1964, though, this same body had voted him out of power.) The Central Committee is a kind of 'parliament of the Party' in which the bloc of local Party bosses (obkom secretaries and secretaries of constituent and autonomous republics) is the strongest group, numbering 146 of the 470 members and candidate members. It is also a very conservative group and was almost certainly opposed to Andropov and Ustinov's anti-corruption stance. The recent dismissal of S. F. Medunov, Krasnodar obkom secretary, had sent a shock wave through the regional Party system. When the obkom secretaries arrived in Moscow for the Plenum on 11 November, they tried to work out a joint stand. But they had too little time to form any real opposition to Andropov, since the Plenum was held the next day. The speed with which the succession was arranged and the decision that Chernenko should be the person to propose Andropov meant that the election took place without any discussion.

The Central Committee meeting started early in the morning of 12 November. The centre of Moscow was sealed off by troops and police for about three hours. Central Committee members from the provinces who arrived that day and who were driven to the Kremlin in official cars could see clearly that the situation was under control.

Andropov chaired the 12 November Plenum and made an introductory speech about Brezhnev's death. This was not the speech of the new General Secretary as many foreign correspondents reported – it was merely the first speech at the Plenum. Contrary to the expectation of many Central Committee members that Andropov would end his speech with a nomination for the post of General Secretary, he concluded with an offer:

> This Plenum has to decide about the election of the General Secretary of the Central Committee of the Communist Party of the Soviet Union. I invite comrades to express their opinions about this question.[1]

The next speaker, 'on behalf of the Politburo', was Chernenko. He made a long speech about Brezhnev, about the Party, about collective leadership, about the economy, and even referred to disarmament. At the very end he proposed that Yuri Andropov, 'who will continue the Brezhnev style of leadership, Brezhnev's care for the interests of the people, Brezhnev's comradely relations with the party cadres', be elected General Secretary.[2]

Andropov's first speech in his capacity as General Secretary and chairman of the Funeral Commission was made at Red Square on Monday morning, 15 November 1982. Soviet state funerals are always carefully staged, and follow a traditional pattern, lasting about two hours even on a cold winter day. There had been two recent state funerals in Red Square – that of Kosygin in December 1980 and that of Suslov in January 1982. Brezhnev's funeral was shorter than those, lasting little more than an hour. It was an unemotional occasion. Andropov made a short introductory speech after which he declared the funeral meeting open. (These words were omitted from the published text, which made Andropov's speech seem part of the event rather than an introduction to the other speeches.) The second speech was made by Dmitri Ustinov and was followed by three short speeches made by representatives of the 'people', one by Academician A. Aleksandrov, President of the Academy of Sciences, the second by a worker, V. V. Pushkarev, and the third by a Party official from Dneprodzerzhinsk, the city in which Brezhnev had started his party work.

The official communiqué about the funeral published the following day claimed: '12 hours 45 minutes. The coffin with the body of the deceased was slowly lowered into the grave.' Surprisingly, this was not true. Instead of being lowered by the customary four military men (Brezhnev was a Marshal and the Supreme Head of the Military Council), there were two plain-clothed funeral attendants. Each held the ends of two lengths of rope and they quickly and clumsily dropped the coffin into the grave. Watching the funeral proceedings live on television in London, I first thought that this was a deliberate symbol. Later I discovered that it was an accidental sign of the shoddiness which penetrated all segments of society during Brezhnev's years in power. It is said that although his coffin was made to normal Kremlin specifications, it was not strong enough to hold a heavy corpse. When the coffin was lifted to be placed on the catafalque for the lying-in-state on 12 November, the bottom collapsed and Brezhnev's body fell through the hole. Within a couple of hours a new metal-plated coffin was produced as a replacement. It was this change that caused the slip which millions of Soviet viewers watched in amazement. The two funeral attendants who had been selected to lower the coffin slowly into the grave suddenly found that the coffin was too heavy for them. One of them could not keep hold of his rope and the coffin dropped. It hit the ground with the sound of an explosion, at the very moment that the first gun salutes shook the air.

Part Two
The Way to the Top

4

Andropov before 1957

It is almost impossible to write anything about Andropov the man. In the Soviet Union people have very little information about Politburo members. They know only as much as is written in the brief official biographies which are published in the Great Soviet Encyclopaedia. Only major figures such as Stalin, Khrushchev and Brezhnev have substantial biographies devoted to them, and even then usually only for as long as they retain their positions. And since these are official biographies, written by special commissions, no personal information is included. Sometimes there are more detailed posthumous biographies of other leaders of Party or state, but this is rare. Most are quickly forgotten or become 'non-persons', as in the case of Trotsky, Bukharin, Rykov, Molotov, Malenkov, Beria, Bulganin and many others who once were in charge of the Soviet Party or government. This is the way the Party is kept pure, unconnected to the mistakes and excesses of particular leaders. New leaders try to legitimize their position by linking themselves directly to Lenin over the heads of their immediate predecessors. It is unlikely that Andropov will continue to present himself to the Soviet public as the man who intends 'to continue the Brezhnev style of leadership' – that style was not very popular.

Members of the Politburo live closed lives and the press never discusses their personal affairs. What little is known about Andropov (that he is a widower, that he speaks English, likes music and French wine and wears strong spectacles, that his daughter is married to an actor of the Tagansky or Mayakovsky theatre and works for the magazine *Theatre*, and that his son is a Soviet delegate to the Madrid follow-up conference of the Conference on Security and Co-operation in Europe) is known from the foreign press. Foreigners who have met Andropov at some occasion or other are not inhibited about reporting these details. All the Soviet people have to go by in their judgement of Politburo members or government ministers are their public appearances, their official speeches, the articles they write or what is known of their actions. Soviet officials are not elected by public ballot, therefore they have no need of publicity campaigns in order to attract potential voters. People know about and become interested in them only after they have assumed some high office.

It will probably be a few years before official Soviet historians write a more detailed and carefully polished biography of Andropov. He first needs to make some impact on domestic and foreign policy so that his actions as the new supreme leader can form the main content of such a book. When news of his appointment was published in Soviet newspapers, the attached brief biographical note told readers very little.[1] There is also a brief formal article in the Soviet Encyclopaedia, and this was used in foreign comments about the new leader.[2]

The Komsomol years

Yuri Vladimirovich Andropov was born on 15 June 1914, the son of a railway worker at the Nagutskaya station in Stavropol province. At the age of sixteen he started work in Mozdok, where he joined the Komsomol. Later he was a boatman on the ships of the Volga transport system, and he also worked as a telegraph operator. He continued his education, probably from 1933 onwards, in a water transport technical college in Rybinsk, in the Yaroslav region, and after graduating from this college in 1936 he stayed on as its full-time Komsomol secretary. The published biography gives no details about Andropov's education beyond mentioning that he had higher (*vysshee*) education. This normally implies graduation from an institute of higher education or a university rather than from a technical school. But if Andropov started his working life at the age of sixteen must have left school after seven or eight years and this would mean that he was not qualified to enter a university or institute of higher education. On the face of it, it would seem that Andropov's education was overstated by the authors of his short published biography. There are some rumours that after his appointment to the KGB he received individual tuition enabling him to graduate from the special 'KGB Academy', which would mean he could claim to have received higher education. However, graduation from this institution, creditable for a military KGB officer, would hardly invite confidence in a political figure.

However, in the case of his professional political career, the post he held in 1940 seems to have been downgraded in the official account. Andropov became the Komsomol organizer of the Volodarsky shipyard in Rybinsk in 1936. All factories and plants which employ more than 1,000 Komsomol members are entitled to a full-time paid Komsomol secretary, and this is a typical starting-point for someone who is embarking upon a professional political career. By 1938 Andropov had been promoted to the post of first secretary of the Yaroslav regional committee (obkom) of the Komsomol. In 1940 he was made first secretary of the Komsomol in the new Karelo-Finnish Union Republic, a position which his official biography refers to merely as the Secretary of Karelia. It was in fact an important and highly sensitive post for the twenty-six-year-old- Andropov. After the 1939–40 Winter War the Soviet Union and Finland signed a peace treaty, on 12 March 1940, under the terms of which Finland ceded part of the Karelian Isthmus, Viborg and other border territories to the USSR. The area was

turned into one of the Union Republics which make up the
Union of Soviet Socialist Republics, and it was Andropov's
task to help to sovietize this new territory. Most Finns, in
fact, did not wish to live there, and were repatriated to
Finland after 1945. Once the 'sovietization' had been completed the republic was again renamed, in 1957, as the
Karelian Autonomous Republic.

Andropov's rapid promotion within the Komsomol was,
in part, due to the Stalinist purges which affected the more
experienced Komsomol cadres in 1937–38. He belongs to
that generation of Soviet leaders who filled the places of
those who disappeared during the Great Terror. For
Brezhnev and Kirilenko this led to rapid promotion in the
Party apparatus. In Andropov's case it brought about his
meteoric rise within the Komsomol.

In 1937 Stalin personally accused the first secretary of the
Central Committee of the All-Union Komsomol, A. V.
Kosarev, and other Komsomol secretaries of not helping the
NKVD to uncover the 'enemies of the people'. Kosarev
argued that there were no enemies amongst the young
Komsomol cadres. Nonetheless he and practically all the
other Komsomol leaders of Moscow and the Ukraine were
soon arrested. A second wave of terror removed Komsomol
leaders, young men in their early thirties, from other
republics and regions. Thus the normal ten years that it
takes for an able Komsomol activist to rise to the regional
secretary level was much reduced in 1938–40. Andropov
became a member of the Communist Party in 1939. This
means that when he was made a regional Komsomol leader
in 1938 he was still only a candidate member of the CPSU –
a clear sign that the previous leadership had been eliminated
and that the new obkom was elected in some haste.

When Germany attacked the Soviet Union in June 1941,
Finland also declared war on the Soviet Union. (This
declaration was not tied to the German declaration, and
Finland capitulated before Germany.) In 1941 Petrozavodsk,
the capital of the Karelo-Finnish Republic, was occupied by

Finnish and German troops. Andropov's official biography indicates that he became an 'active participant in the partisan movement in Karelia from the first days of the Great Patriotic War'.[3] This sentence would normally be interpreted as meaning that he was involved in underground work behind the German and Finnish lines, although this is not stated directly. In 1942 Andropov published an article, 'We will defend you, our Karelia', in the Moscow Komsomol magazine *Smena*,[4] in which he describes the activities of the Karelian partisans and the role of the unoccupied part of the republic in assisting the front. In 1943 a similar though rather more general article appeared in *Komsomol'skaya Pravda*[5] about love for one's native land. From the context of these articles it seems probable that Andropov was actually in Belomorsk at the time, a town north of Petrozavodsk not occupied by German or Finnish troops. It is apparent that the headquarters of the Karelian partisans were situated on the Soviet side of the front line, where the supplies were kept, and Andropov was probably in charge of the organizational and political aspect of some of the partisan operations from this command post. It is clear that he was able to move to other parts of the country when necessary, probably to Murmansk, connected to Belomorsk by rail, and to Arkhangelsk. There is no record of his participation in any actual combat missions in Karelia.

Andropov's Party career dates from the capitulation of Finland and the liberation of Petrozavodsk in 1944. He became the Second Secretary of the Petrozavodsk Party Committee. By 1947 he had been promoted to Second Secretary of the Karelo-Finnish Republican Party organization. The First Secretary of that organization was Otto Kuusinen, an old Bolshevik who was a Finn by nationality. It was Kuusinen, apparently, who suggested Andropov's promotion to work in the Central Committee apparatus, and who later recommended him for diplomatic appointment. In 1951 he became first an inspector and then head of a section of a department of the Central Committee.

Although it is not known exactly which departments he worked in, from an article he published in *Pravda* at this time it is clear that he was mainly concerned with the timber and cellulose industry.[6] Very soon afterwards he was sent to Hungary, first as Counsellor and in 1954 as Ambassador.

Ambassador to Hungary

If it had not been for the Hungarian uprising in October and November 1956, Andropov might well have remained a diplomat. He took his ambassadorial work very seriously and was probably unique amongst Soviet ambassadors because he studied the Hungarian language and could speak it quite well. This made his relations with Hungarian leaders much easier.

Although it is thought that Kuusinen recommended Andropov for diplomatic work, no details are known about his promotion. The American columnist Joseph Kraft insists that my brother, Roy Medvedev, told him that

> Georgi Malenkov, who had succeeded Stalin as Premier and Party Secretary, had to fight a battle with Khrushchev for control of the Party organization. To strengthen his position, Malenkov wanted to dislodge the Party Secretary in the Lithuanian Republic. Andropov was designated to report on the man, and Malenkov gave him to understand that he wanted a bad report. Instead, Andropov gave the Lithuanian Party Secretary a clean bill of health. As punishment, Malenkov exiled Andropov to Budapest.[7]

I would be extremely surprised if Roy were the source of this and other stories that Kraft attributes to him.[8] As the author of a book on Khrushchev, Roy is well aware that Malenkov did not succeed Stalin as Party Secretary and that there was no fight between them 'to control the Party organization'. In fact, Roy states that immediately after Stalin's death

> . . . it was generally agreed that Khrushchev should con-

centrate on his work as Secretary of the Central Committee
. . . he took charge of the entire Secretariat of the Central
Committee, although the post of First Secretary had not yet
been formally instituted.[9]

In any case, the position of Ambassador to a Soviet bloc
country ranked higher than Andropov's prior position in
the Party apparatus, and thus represented promotion rather
than demotion. It was only later that appointment as
Ambassador became a form of punishment and exile, and
even then the countries chosen were smaller and more
distant.

The official biography tells us very little about Andropov's
years in Hungary, but émigré Hungarian and Russian
sources have a great deal to say about his role in the suppres-
sion of the Hungarian revolt. It is more than likely that they
exaggerate the part he played. The whole Hungarian operation was under the close personal control of Khrushchev,
who sent two special emissaries to Hungary, Suslov and
Mikoyan. The military part of the operation was commanded by Marshals Ivan Konev and Zhukov while
General Serov, head of the KGB, who had much experience
of military counter-intelligence, was in charge of the KGB
activity. Nonetheless Andropov, as the man on the spot,
knew the local situation much better than the others, and he
must have played some part in the events. His response to
the situation in Hungary can be deduced from the fact that
he was promoted after the uprising had been suppressed. It
is out of the question that he could have displayed any
sympathy for the Hungarian revolutionaries (or 'counter-
revolutionaries' as they were called by the Soviet authorities).

In 1953, when Andropov was appointed to the Soviet
Embassy in Hungary, and in 1954 when he was promoted to
Ambassador, the Minister of Foreign Affairs in the Soviet
Union was still Vyacheslav Molotov, a conservative Stalinist
figure. Soviet Ambassadors to socialist countries have their

contacts in the Central Committee, but officially they report and receive instructions through the Ministry of Foreign Affairs. Molotov was dismissed from his position late in 1955, and Dmitri Shepilov was appointed in his stead. Shepilov, a moderately liberal figure, was one of Khrushchev's protégés, but in 1957 he joined forces with Molotov, Malenkov and Kaganovich, to form the anti-Khrushchev group in the Party Presidium which tried to topple the leader. He believed the plot had some chance of success, and had been promised the position of Prime Minister. When it failed, he was dismissed from high office and became Director of the Institute of Economy of the Kirghiz Academy of Sciences in Frunze, where at the time of writing he still works. Shepilov's departure left his old post open for Andrei Gromyko, the most durable figure in Soviet foreign affairs.

When Andropov became Ambassador to Hungary in 1954, Matyas Rákosi, leader of the Hungarian Communist Party during the 1949–51 terror, had recently been dismissed. Rákosi was a staunch disciple of Stalin who had spent many years in Moscow during the twenties and thirties. An associate of Bela Kun, leader of the short-lived 1919 Communist government in Hungary, he was compromised by Beria's trial in 1953 and was removed from his office of Premier as a result. However he still retained considerable power within the Hungarian Communist Party. He was replaced as Premier by Imre Nagy, who immediately began to slow down the pace of collectivization, which was extremely unpopular in Hungary, and to emphasize the need to produce more consumer goods. Shortly before the Twentieth Congress of the CPSU, Rákosi managed to regain his position, and Nagy was dismissed. It was this event that polarized the people of Hungary and led to the formation of a strong opposition. Rákosi found it increasingly difficult to carry on and the leadership began to disintegrate.

The Hungarian revolt was a direct consequence of Khrushchev's secret speech at the Twentieth Party Congress in February 1956 in which he denounced Stalin's terror, particularly insofar as it was directed against the party cadres. The circumstances of the preparation of this speech – in secret because of the objections of Malenkov, Molotov, Voroshilov, Kaganovich and some other members of the Party Presidium – meant that Khrushchev could not prepare foreign Communist leaders for the new policy line. Although he was already strong enough to carry out some measure of de-Stalinization in the USSR, the other socialist countries were still largely headed by typical Stalinists. Most of them (in Bulgaria, Hungary, Romania, Czechoslovakia, Poland and Albania) had organized their own campaigns of terror in 1949–51 (with the help of the MGB), in the course of which they had eliminated their rivals, Communists who had distinguished themselves during the war as leaders of the resistance and had become national heroes. Khrushchev's speech produced political crises in all these countries, but in Hungary the crises developed into open revolt.

Khrushchev's speech was a disaster for Rákosi, because by implication it exposed his own crimes against Hungarian party cadres. A limited rehabilitation of some of the victims of Rákosi's terror was unavoidable. Amongst those earlier released from prison was János Kádár, who had been jailed for 'Titoism'. There were very strong feelings against Rákosi and he was forced to resign in August 1956. E. Gëro became Party First Secretary, and shortly afterwards Rákosi fled to Moscow, in fear for his life. In the Soviet Union popular feeling about Hungary and Romania was rather negative in 1956: the fact that both had been German allies during the war was still resented. Romania had capitulated in 1944 and had even gone as far as declaring war against Germany, but Hungary, occupied by German troops, had put up much greater resistance to Soviet 'liberation' with the result that the Red Army lost about a million soldiers there in 1944–45. The fact that these losses had taken place because of the German occupation, which had imposed enormous hardship on the Hungarians themselves, seemed irrelevant.

Rákosi's resignation did not silence the opposition, which called for Nagy's return to power. Even when the rebels got their way and Nagy was once again appointed Prime Minister, popular ferment did not die down. Nagy appointed a coalition government and Hungary was declared to be a multi-party state. It was probably at this point that Soviet intervention became inevitable. When he was informed that additional Soviet troops had crossed the border, Nagy declared Hungary's neutrality, announced its withdrawal from the Warsaw Pact, and appealed for help to the United Nations. But by then the die was cast.

Within the Soviet Union Khrushchev's position had been undermined rather than strengthened by his speech at the Twentieth Party Congress. He did not have full control over either the Party Presidium or the Central Committee, and the crises in Poland and Hungary in the autumn increased opposition to the de-Stalinization which he had initiated. Malenkov, Molotov and Kaganovich openly accused him of having damaged the international Communist movement irreparably. The Chinese Communist Party echoed this accusation. The loss of Soviet influence in Poland and Hungary would be a strategic disaster, and unless the crises there were resolved, Khrushchev realized, he was bound to lose his position. In Poland Gomulka managed to convince the Soviet leadership (which arrived *en masse* to prevent his election as Party leader) that the Polish Communist Party retained control. The situation in Hungary was less certain and Andropov's prognosis was pessimistic. The new movement had all the signs of a popular social-democratic revolution. Moreover, American propaganda broadcast via Radio Free Europe from Munich promised military help to the rebels (an empty promise, as it turned out).

Before Khrushchev could intervene in Hungary, prominent figures had to be found who would agree to form a new government. Mikoyan and Suslov were sent to Budapest to co-operate with Andropov in this quest. Khrushchev also wanted the agreement of all the Soviet Union's major allies on the necessity of intervention. Liu Shao-Chi, China's deputy head of state, flew to Moscow to press for action. The Romanian, Czech, Bulgarian and Polish leaders also urged military intervention. Soon even Marshal Tito gave his blessing. Zhukov, the Minister of Defence, moved several divisions and an army of tanks up to the Hungarian border. Some Soviet military units were already in Hungary – they had been stationed there since the war. On 4 November the Soviet army moved into Budapest. A new Hungarian government was formed under the leadership of János Kádár, Antal Apro and Ferenc Münnich. The revolt was crushed.

There are several stories in circulation about Andropov's hypocritical behaviour during the crucial days of October and November 1956. The one which is most often heard is that he invited General Pál Maléter, the Hungarian Minister of Defence, to a banquet on the night of 3 November with a promise of negotiation. During the dinner, the Soviet KGB Chairman Ivan Serov stormed into the banqueting hall with his men and arrested the entire Hungarian delegation.[10] When news of Andropov's succession became known on 12 November 1982, this story was repeated many times.[11] However, it is a fabrication, for the episode it relates never took place. More reliable studies of the Hungarian uprising show that Maléter was arrested at the Soviet military headquarters on 3 November 1956.[12] He was taking part in discussions with General M. S. Malinin, Commander-in-Chief of the Soviet forces in Hungary,

> who appeared to be negotiating in good faith, and to be taken by surprise when, shortly after midnight, the talks were suddenly interrupted by armed KGB officers – by some accounts, personally led by the head of the KGB, General Ivan Serov – and Maléter and his colleagues were arrested.[13]

Contrary to rumour, Pál Maléter was not shot after arrest but was tried secretly and executed in 1958. This was announced in a Hungarian Government communiqué and reported in *The Times* on 17 June 1958; on 18 June *The Times* carried an editorial condemning the executions, as well as an obituary. This means that János Kádár and Ferenc Münnich, his first deputy and the minister in charge of the armed forces and security in Hungary at the time, were directly responsible for Maléter's trial and execution. If they had to get approval from Moscow, it was Khrushchev they consulted, not Andropov.

It is not easy to reconstruct Andropov's actions at the beginning of November. There are many conflicting stories. However, it is known that he was inside Budapest when Soviet troops began to break through the city's perimeter defence. He visited Imre Nagy, to assure him that the Soviet Union had no aggressive intentions and to try to prevent the Hungarian government from taking any active defensive measures which could lead to bloodshed. However General Béla Király, military commander of Budapest during the revolution, offers a different explanation for Andropov's unexpected visit to Nagy. Király himself was attempting to persuade Nagy to offer resistance to the Russian forces. According to his story:

> The first time I called him, Imre Nagy told me the whole affair was an absurd mistake. 'Soviet Ambassador Andropov is here in my office', he said, 'and he is trying to contact Moscow to ask for instructions. He is of the opinion that someone has made a tragic mistake, and he is trying to stop the slaughter'. Up to the last minute Imre Nagy believed that he was not witnessing an act of infamy, but an unintentional disaster.
>
> The Soviet Ambassador's presence in the Prime Minister's office at the very hour of his government's vicious attack is comparable to the presence of the Japanese mission in the USA at the time of Pearl Harbor. But Andropov's case was perhaps even more monstrous. In a state of revolution such as there was in Budapest during this 'winter in November', there was every chance that terrified, frustrated, and outraged revolutionaries might seize the Ambassador and put

him to death. What a sensational opportunity this would have been for Soviet propaganda! It is my opinion that this may have been precisely why the Soviet government ordered the Ambassador to go to the Parliament building, just as it opened its offensive against Hungary. The USSR might have lost a diplomat but it would have gained an inestimable propaganda weapon with which to denounce the 'barbaric Hungarians' whom the 'civilized Russians' wanted to teach 'law and order'.[14]

Király's interpretation is probably wrong: it would be more natural to suppose that the Soviet military command genuinely wanted to avoid bloodshed.

The account in *The Times* of 13 November 1982 maintains that 'Andropov issued more safe conducts a month later, to lure the Prime Minister, Imre Nagy, and his ministers from their refuge at the Yugoslav Embassy'. This statement is also incorrect. Nagy left the embassy after receiving a written guarantee of safe conduct from János Kádár. It is possible that Andropov knew that this guarantee would not be honoured, but the whole operation of Nagy's arrest was apparently planned at the level of Kádár, Münnich and Khrushchev. The episode seriously damaged Soviet–Yugoslav relations and enraged Marshal Tito. Andropov probably knew what was going to happen, but Hungary was an occupied country and the Soviet army was in control. Major operations, like the arrest of Nagy, could not have been undertaken without a personal directive from Khrushchev or from the Soviet Party Presidium.

Andropov worked together with the military commanders and the representatives of the KGB, and during his final months in Hungary – November 1956 to March 1957 – there were certainly tens of thousands of arrests. However, the trials and executions which terrorized the Hungarian population did not begin until after his return to Moscow. As head of the foreign relations (socialist) department of the Central Committee, he continued to have some responsibility for the events in Hungary. However, there are rumours that he suffered a heart attack[15] in March 1957, which was the immediate cause of his replacement as Soviet Ambassador.

Khrushchev's own account of the Hungarian revolt does not mention Andropov by name at all. He describes the mission of Suslov and Mikoyan, the role of Marshal Konev and the discussions in the Party Presidium and with the leaders of allied countries. This suggests that Andropov did not report directly to Khrushchev, but to Suslov and Mikoyan. Rákosi's dismissal in July 1956 was probably based on advice from the Soviet Embassy, but Mikoyan was sent to supervise the Hungarian Central Committee meeting. Gëro was made First Secretary at this meeting, but it soon became clear that this was a mistake. He proved incapable of dealing with the situation and was replaced by Kádár.

Andropov remained in Hungary for several months after the revolt had been crushed. It is possible that during 1957 he discussed the Hungarian situation personally with Khrushchev, since, as Khrushchev tells us in his memoirs, he made a number of secret trips to Hungary in 1957 'at the behest of the Hungarian government and the Hungarian Central Committee'.[16]

5

Andropov as a Central Committee Secretary

In 1957 Andropov returned to Moscow to head the Central Committee Foreign Affairs department which deals with socialist countries. Although his role in Hungary in 1956 must have advanced his standing in the eyes of Mikoyan, Suslov and Khrushchev and contributed to his promotion, this was not the only reason for his new position. In June 1957 Khrushchev had narrowly survived an attempt to unseat him by Molotov, Malenkov, Kaganovich, Shepilov and Voroshilov. Once the anti-Party Group (as Khrushchev's opponents were called) had been defeated, there was a shake-up within the Party apparatus and their supporters were dismissed. Andropov's old friend Otto Kuusinen was once again promoted to full membership of the Party Presidium, and he sponsored Adropov's promotion. Moreover, the events in Eastern Europe in 1956 and the increasing conflict with China and Albania had made it clear that the section of the Central Committee Secretariat which dealt with relations with the socialist countries had to be strengthened. What was needed was a special group composed of competent experts on each of the socialist countries to advise the Central Committee on policy.

Very little is known about Andropov's work in this department between 1957 and 1962. In part this is because the department itself was at a formative stage. But it is also a question of Khrushchev's fondness for personal diplomacy without any consultation. Although the Chinese section of the department grew rapidly, it is difficult to believe that

Khrushchev's sudden decision to recall all Soviet technical experts from China in 1960 was made on the basis of informed advice from the relevant Central Committee department. It is more likely to have been the result of personal impulse, translated into an unreasonable directive. The only information about Andropov's career at that time is that he was elected to the Central Committee at the Twenty-Second Party Congress in 1961.

My own interest in Andropov as a politician began in 1963, the year in which Lysenko launched a new offensive against his critics. (Lysenko, the President of the Lenin Academy of Agricultural Sciences, was a pseudoscientist who rejected all modern theories in genetics, but who nontheless enjoyed the support of both Stalin and Khrushchev because of his promise of easy success in agriculture.) I had been very critical of Lysenko's domination of biology, genetics and agriculture in a book which I wrote in 1962, *Biological Science and the 'Personality Cult'*.[1] This book was widely circulated in *samizdat*. As a result of extreme pressure from the administration and Party committee of the Moscow Agricultural Academy, where I was employed as a senior research scientist, I was forced to resign and move to a job in one of the new institutes of the Medical Academy in Obninsk in the Kaluga region. When the Moscow Party secretary, Nikolai Yegorychev, attacked me personally as well as my book at a Plenum meeting on ideology in May 1963, an attempt was made to persuade the Medical Academy too to dismiss me. The year 1963 was a disastrous one for agriculture, and many geneticists were threatened with dismissal. Khrushchev's advisers on agriculture, all of them protégés or supporters of Lysenko, blamed the agricultural failures on those scientists who resisted Lysenko's ideas. Khrushchev had inherited from Stalin a tendency to seek scapegoats for his own mistakes. Scientists who were implicated in these polemics sought to find anti-Lysenko officials amongst the upper echelons of the Party. My own chief protector was Professor V. D.

Timakov, Vice-President of the Academy of Medical Sciences, who played an important role in the revival of medical genetics in the Soviet Union, a subject which had been forbidden between 1937 and 1956. He told me that Andropov, then a secretary of the Central Committee, was opposed to Lysenko's influence and that he had made some discreet gestures in support of genetic research in the Soviet Union.

The idea of a secretary of the Central Committee with an interest in genetics is not as far-fetched as it might seem. It was not that Andropov was, or pretended to be, an expert in the subject. But as head of the Central Committee of the foreign affairs department for socialist countries, he had already had a first encounter with the genetics controversy in his dealings with Czechoslovakia. The founder of classical genetics and the main target of Lysenko's criticism was Gregor Mendel, born in Brno, which was an Austrian town in the nineteenth century but is now in Czechoslovakia. Mendel was a source of great pride to all Czechs, and when Mendelism became a term of abuse in the Soviet lexicon and the Czechs were forced to close the Mendel Museum in Brno and remove the monument to Mendel in the town square in 1948, the genetics controversy became a sensitive national political issue. Early in the sixties the United Nations declared that 1965, the centenary of Mendel's most important discoveries, would be a Mendel Centennial jubilee. The Czech Academy of Sciences reopened the Mendel Museum, and the white marble monument was returned triumphantly to its former location well in advance of the international Centennial symposium which was to take place in Brno. Lysenko and his supporters accused the Czechs of 'ideological diversion' and Andropov became involved as an intermediary between the Czech and the Soviet leaderships. Andropov was, it seems, in favour of giving the Czechs a free hand to celebrate the Mendel centenary. This was done in April–May 1964, although the Soviet Academy of Sciences was instructed to boycott the symposium. This would have been a humiliation for the Czechs, but in October 1964 Khrushchev was dismissed, Lysenko's influence diminished immediately and the Soviet Academy of Sciences decided to participate in the activities of the Centennial, even laying a wreath on the monument in Brno. On 24 June, 1965 *Pravda* published a first-rate article on Mendel, and other Soviet newspapers followed suit on the following day.

In view of the fact that Andropov was virtually unknown to the general public in 1962–63, it was extremely unexpected when Khrushchev selected him in 1964 for the great privilege of making the traditional Lenin Day Speech, a partly theoretical, partly political address at the annual meeting of the top Party and state organizations on Lenin's birthday, 22 April. The speech is normally published in all Soviet newspapers on 23 April, with a photograph of the speaker.[2] This was Andropov's first major political address, and he naturally included it later among his collected speeches.[3] The version published in 1979 was not identical to the 1964 original. In the original there are, of course, many paragraphs in praise of Khrushchev's policies; in the later, 'doctored' version all mention of Khrushchev's name has been excised and some paragraphs have been rewritten to remove all possible association with his actions. This practice of altering articles and speeches in retrospect was begun many years ago. Neither Lenin's nor Stalin's nor Khrushchev's *Collected Works* contain the text of every speech exactly as it was delivered, for a number have been 'doctored' to remove or alter statements which have since become embarrassing. (Lenin, of course, did not perform the task himself: a special committee undertook it 'on his behalf'. Other leaders take personal responsibility for alterations.) With the Lenin Day Speech, the first of three that he has since delivered, Andropov became a public figure.

In October 1964 my brother, Roy Medvedev, began producing a monthly typewritten clandestine magazine, *Political Diary*. I assisted him in this endeavour and kept a top copy of the magazine which I microfilmed. We prepared seventy-nine between 1964 and 1971.[4] The journal began with an attempt to analyse political trends within the Soviet leadership and in the Soviet Union, and for this we needed to follow both official and unofficial discussions very closely. (Later we began to include *samizdat* materials.) The first issue concentrated on the Plenum which dismissed Khrushchev. The main report was made by Suslov, no debate was allowed and the recommendation of the Presidium for his dismissal was passed without comment. Although Andropov was a prominent figure at the Plenum, he was not very influential. The Central Committee prepared a confidential letter of explanation about Khrushchev's departure and this was sent to the leaders of Communist Parties abroad. This letter was not difficult to prepare, since his fall came about as the result of administrative blunders and economic mismanagement, rather than disagreements about the substance of international policy or problems of de-Stalinization. Although the Plenum did not introduce many changes, there were some positive moves. Lysenko's fall was immediate and very welcome. Adzhubei, Khrushchev's son-in-law and editor of *Izvestiya*, and Pavel Satukov, editor of *Pravda* and a Khrushchev supporter, were both dismissed. Satukov was replaced by Aleksei Rumyantsev, the editor of *Problems of Peace and Socialism*, the international Communist journal published in Prague. As the official organ of the Soviet bloc, *Problems of Peace and Socialism* was under Andropov's direct control, and it was probably Andropov who recommended the promotion of Rumyantsev, a good journalist with fairly independent views whose articles in *Pravda* were always carefully read and discussed.

Andropov's political future was somewhat insecure at this time, particularly since all the main Party functionaries were due for re-election at the Twenty-Third Party Congress. He had been elected to the Central Committee at the Twenty-Second Congress, the most radical Congress in the history of the Party, in the course of which Stalin was declared to have been a criminal and his body ordered to be removed from the Mausoleum in Red Square. Andropov's appointment as a secretary of the Central Committee in 1962 was his most important step towards the inner circles of power. He had supported Khrushchev's political reforms but, fortunately for him, as head of the foreign department of the Central Committee, he was not directly involved in Soviet domestic economic policies and therefore carried no responsibility for Khrushchev's economic failures. But he was viewed as a strong anti-Stalinist and he seemed to be an outsider in the Central Committee Secretariat, belonging neither to the Brezhnev group nor to the technocrats grouped around Kosygin nor to the Shelepin–Suslov alliance. If the latter, conservative group managed to dominate the Twenty-Third, Congress, Andropov's chances of reappointment as a Central Committee secretary would be slight. This probably explains his discreet attempts to mobilize prominent intellectuals to influence the actions taken by the Congress.

There were many signs in 1965 that a process of 're-Stalinization' was a possibility. On the eve of the twentieth anniversary of the victory over Nazi Germany, articles eulogizing Stalin appeared in the Soviet press.[5] For anyone with an understanding of the censorship system in the USSR this clearly indicated that a directive had been issued from the propaganda department of the Central Committee. In August the writers Andrei Sinyavsky and Yulii Daniel were arrested. Their clumsy 'open' trial in January 1966 had an extremely depressing effect on the Soviet intellectual community – it was this trial that began what later became known as the dissident movement. There seemed to be some disagreement between those high Party officials who wanted to rehabilitate Stalin and others who were against this trend. Brezhnev's position was not yet well established and his power was limited. Although he was against the full rehabilitation of Stalin, he had halted the process of de-Stalinization. Stalin's name began to appear in the official press more and more frequently, almost always in a positive context. There was no further rehabilitation of his victims or criticism of his rule.

A further sign that the political situation was serious occurred in September 1965 when Rumyantsev was dismissed from his position at *Pravda* in retaliation for a very liberal article entitled 'Party and Intelligentsia' which he had written for it with the assistance of Yuri Karyakin. Karyakin, previously a journalist in Prague working for *Problems of Peace and Socialism*, in which he had published some good articles, including a thoughtful analysis of Solzhenitsyn's *One Day in the Life of Ivan Denisovich*,[6] had arrived in Moscow at the beginning of 1965 to take quite a lowly position as instructor in Andropov's department of the Central Commitee apparatus. After a few months he was given a much more responsible job on *Pravda*, as assistant to the newly-appointed editor, Rumyantsev. He became friendly with Solzhenitsyn, Roy Medvedev, Pyotr Yakir and other dissidents. In September Solzhenitsyn's papers, including the three sole copies of *The First Circle*, were confiscated. Solzhenitsyn was in despair until he recalled that he had given one copy to Yuri Karyakin for safe keeping – it was extremely unlikely that the KGB would raid the offices of *Pravda*. Much later, in his autobiographical book *The Oak and the Calf*, Solzhenitsyn described how Karyakin saved the manuscript and returned it to the author when it was needed. But by the time Solzhenitsyn wrote this, his attitude to both Karyakin and Rumyantsev had changed: 'Like a child I put my faith in Y. Karyakin and his specious assurances that his oh, so very liberal boss, Rumyantsev, now editor of *Pravda,* was thinking of publishing one or two innocuous chapters of *The First Circle.*'[7] When Rumyansev was dismissed from *Pravda*, Karyakin also lost his job. Rumyantsev, a Central Committee member, was later appointed director of the Institute of Sociology and elected Vice-President of the Academy of Sciences of the USSR. Karyakin became a researcher at the Institute of the Inter-

national Workers' Movement and began to write liberal–
Marxist articles, mostly for *samizdat*. A speech he made at a
meeting in memory of Andrei Platonov, a gifted writer who
died in prison camp, was circulated in *samizdat*, and as a
result Karyakin was expelled from the Party. Later this
measure was commuted into a 'strong reprimand with
warning'. [8]

There were rumours in Moscow in the autumn of 1965
that a change of leadership was about to take place. These
rumours were in part related to the forthcoming Central
Committee Plenum which was to consider 'organizational
problems', a euphemism for personnel changes. Brezhnev's
position was weak. He had been appointed First Secretary in
1964 as a compromise figure and because he had officially
held the second position in the Party since 1963, acting as
chairman of the Party Presidium when Khrushchev was away
on his frequent journeys. Khrushchev had never doubted
Brezhnev's loyalty. Brezhnev was also Chairman of the
Presidium of the Supreme Soviet (nominal head of state) at
that time, a position taken over by Anastas Mikoyan in June
1964, when Brezhnev became a full-time Central Committee
Secretary, the *de facto* 'second' secretary. Since Khrushchev's
dismissal was not immediately followed by a purge of his
followers, Brezhnev assumed the post which Khrushchev had
vacated. However, when Khrushchev's reorganizations of
the Party and state apparatus were reversed in 1965, criticism of Khrushchev within the Party intensified, and
Brezhnev was implicated. As Chairman of the Presidium of
the Supreme Soviet, he had never objected to Khrushchev's
more dubious reforms, which the Supreme Soviet had
obediently endorsed. Moreover, it was Brezhnev who
delivered the main address at the ceremony to celebrate
Khrushchev's seventieth birthday in April 1964. He had not
taken a direct part in the plot against Khrushchev. Suslov
and Shelepin, who had played the key roles, did not trust
him, and waited until he left Moscow on 5 October, as head
of the official delegation sent to celebrate the fifteenth anni-

versay of the German Democratic Republic. Khrushchev was at his summer residence on the Black Sea, and Mikoyan, Chairman of the Presidium of the Supreme Soviet, was also on holiday. Suslov briefly held the Party leadership, and the Council of Ministers was in Kosygin's control. Vladimir Semichastny, a friend and protégé of Shelepin, was in charge of the KGB. The military had many complaints against Khrushchev, and Marshal Malinovsky, Minister of Defence, supported the Suslov–Shelepin plot. By the time Brezhnev returned to Moscow, the majority of the Party Presidium had already expressed their support for the conspiracy and several key Central Committee members, obkom secretaries, had been invited to join it. Brezhnev therefore, who was not in fact against the plot, had little choice but to give it his support. By the time Khrushchev and Mikoyan returned from the south, a temporary distribution of posts had already been decided upon and it was this that made the dismissal so easy. But by 1965 it was time to make the 1964 interim decisions permanent, and this gave rise to a power struggle within the leadership.

The October 1964 Plenum had decreed that seventy was to be the retirement age for the leadership. Accordingly, Mikoyan notified the Party Presidium that he would retire in 1965. There was a rumour (or perhaps a deliberate leak) that Brezhnev would replace him as Chairman of the Presidium of the Supreme Soviet. It was expected that either Suslov or Shelepin would assume the Party leadership. Shelepin was supported by L. F. Illichev, the most conservative member of the Party Presidium and a neo-Stalinist. He also had strong support from the KGB because during his brief spell as its head (1958–61) he had given many of his friends jobs in that organization. Shelepin also controlled the Ministry of Internal Affairs and the Committee of Party and State Control, the body which supplemented the KGB in dealing with Party affairs. He had formerly been in charge of the Komsomol and had put many friends into important positions in television, radio, the Committee on the film industry, TASS and other organizations. In addition he had the support of many of the younger officials in the Party apparatus. Although Suslov was the most experienced Party *apparatchik,* he had not yet become its 'Chief Ideologue'. Illichev was at that time more prominent in the field of ideology, while Suslov had considerable power in foreign affairs.

In this power struggle, Andropov would lose no matter who emerged the victor. If Shelepin won, his chances of political survival were minimal. With Suslov in charge, he might retain his position but no more than that. He decided to back Brezhnev, whose lack of ambition and somewhat ineffectual personality would suit his ends. Moreover, they were neighbours in the custom-built apartment block for Party functionaries on Kutuzovsky prospekt.

Intellectual circles in Moscow were well aware of the power struggle in the Presidium and wanted neither Suslov nor Shelepin to come out on top. Suslov was associated with the possibility of re-Stalinization, but although Shelepin was known to be anti-Stalinist, it was clear that he also had ambitions to be the new 'great leader'. His KGB background and his collaboration with the KGB in the 1964–66 trials of Brodsky, Sinyavsky and Daniel made him unpopular. Solzhenitsyn, in his autobiography, evokes the fears experienced by the Soviet intelligentsia at that time:

> . . . we can say with near certainty that what was planned was an abrupt return to Stalinism, with 'Iron Shurik' Shelepin in the lead: he wanted, so they say, to tighten up the economy and the administration, Stalin fashion, and on this he is supposed to have been at odds with Kosygin; but on the need for a tighter ideological line not one of them disagreed . . . What, the Stalinists inquired, had been the point of overthrowing Khrushchev if not to revert to Stalinism? No one knows all the steps the Shelepinites had in mind. But one step they took successfully: the arrest of Sinyavsky and Daniel at the beginning of September 1965. (Semichastny's

henchmen were calling for the arrest of 'a thousand intellectuals' in Moscow.)[9]

The confiscation of Solzhenitsyn's papers and manuscripts
in September 1965 had an even more depressing effect than
the arrest of Sinyavsky and Daniel. The latter were 'secret'
writers who had published their works abroad under
pseudonyms and were not known to the general public.
Solzhenitsyn had already become a symbol of anti-Stalinism
in literature.

It seemed, after the Plenum preceding the Twenty-Third
Congress, that Suslov was winning the power struggle.
Illichev was dismissed and a newcomer, Pyotr Demichev,
was put in charge of ideological work. Since Demichev was
an expert on chemical machinery, he was clearly incapable
of dealing with ideological problems and this meant that he
would work under Suslov's full supervision. The Party
Presidium took an unprecedented decision to ban independent speeches by members of the Presidium at the Party
Congress. The official report, delivered by Brezhnev as First
Secretary, would have to reflect a joint view. In this way
both mutual criticism and competitive performances would
be avoided. This decision was not to the advantage of
Shelepin, a good speaker, but helpful to Suslov who was
well known as a bore. Podgorny's election to Mikoyan's
post of Chairman of the Presidium of the Supreme Soviet
improved Brezhnev's chances of survival. Suslov was going
to have to be satisfied with the role of king-maker.

In February 1966 a prominent Moscow journalist,
Semyon Rostovsky (better known as Ernst Henry), wrote a
well argued appeal against re-Stalinization, addressing it to
the Twenty-Third Party Congress. He collected the signa-
tures of twenty-five prominent figures from the world of
science and the arts, including Pyotr Kapitsa, Andrei
Sakharov, Igor Tamm, Ivan Maisky, Konstantin Paustovsky,
Maya Plisetskaya and Mikhail Romm; later more than one
hundred other prominent individuals signed a second copy

which was also delivered to the Central Committee. Ernst Henry had no difficulty in persuading people to sign the letter since he claimed to be taking this step on behalf of influential anti-Stalinist Central Committee members whose position at the Congress would be strengthened if the major figures of Soviet art and science expressed themselves against re-Stalinization. Andropov was one of the 'unofficial sponsors' claimed by Ernst Henry, and junior employees in his department tried, in a discreet way, to confirm this. This letter was circulated amongst Central Committee members and seems to have had the desired effect. Stalin's name was not mentioned at the Twenty-Third Party Congress. At the same time there were only vague references to the Twenty-Second Party Congress where the most explicit condemnation of Stalinism had taken place. The whole problem of Stalin and his victims was simply shelved. It has remained shelved to this day. Ernst Henry himself is now known to have been a professional intelligence agent prior to 1947. He worked in Germany before 1934, and then in Britain, where it was rumoured that he had connections with Guy Burgess and Donald Maclean.[19] Whether this is true or not, he was apparently friendly with Maclean in Moscow. When he returned to the Soviet Union from Britain he was arrested, and was only released after Stalin's death.

Suslov was the main organizer of the Twenty-Third Party Congress and this enabled him to influence the composition of the new Central Committee. By the time the Congress came to an end Shelepin's chances of becoming leader had diminished and Suslov had become the second most important man in the Party. Because the crucial struggle was between Suslov and Shelepin, Brezhnev not only survived but improved his position. Kosygin and Podgorny were both on his side, since a weak and unambitious First Secretary made their own standing in the leadership more secure. They formed a triumvirate, and Suslov became the 'Chief Ideologue', second in the Party hierarchy but only fourth in the leadership. The position of First Secretary was redesignated General Secretary and the Party Presidium once again became the Politburo. These semantic changes were considered to be a concession to the Stalinists and a warning to the general public, for both terms were closely associated with Stalin's rule. The title General Secretary had been changed to First Secretary after his death, while Stalin himself had changed the Politburo into the Party Presidium in 1952 at the Nineteenth Party Congress.

The danger of neo-Stalinism was thus not over. In fact, the most serious attempt to rehabilitate Stalin was made in October 1966 at an All-Union Conference of 'ideological workers', attended by about 1,000 obkom secretaries, secretaries of the Union Republics, chief editors of the main newspapers and magazines and other relevant officials.[11] Between sixty and seventy per cent of those present applauded when Stalin was praised. Liberal magazines like *Novy Mir* and *Yunnost'* were criticized. The Chairman of the KGB made a speech attempting to justify the severe sentences awarded at the Sinyavsky–Daniel trial (seven years' imprisonment) and warning intellectuals to behave properly in future. Andropov also made a speech at this conference, but he restricted himself to talking about the Sino–Soviet conflict and about Soviet relations with Romania, Cuba and other countries.

Andropov was soon to have far more to do with the problem of the intellectuals. Brezhnev was determined to reduce Shelepin's influence further, and in particular, his control of the KGB through his friend Semichastny. In 1967 Semichastny provided excellent grounds for his dismissal from the post of Chairman of the KGB. To everyone's surprise, Andropov was appointed as his successor.

6

Andropov becomes Head of the KGB

Andropov's appointment to the KGB was originally considered an optimistic sign. In a comment on the event, Roy Medvedev wrote:

> Andropov has been appointed minister of the KGB. He was previously in charge of the Central Committee Department on socialist countries and a Secretary of the Central Committee. He has the reputation of being a clever, intelligent man with sound common sense. The fact that he has simultaneously been promoted to candidate membership of the Politburo shows that he has been given much wider powers.[1]

In the Party hierarchy the KGB chairmanship is lower than the rank of Secretary of the Central Committee and Andropov was probably made a candidate member of the Politburo to compensate. His new position in the Party also made him independent of Shelepin. Had he remained completely outside the Politburo, he would have been answerable to Shelepin, since all non-Politburo officials are subordinate to a member of the Politburo. As a candidate member of the Politburo, Andropov was under Brezhnev's direct control.

The reasons for Semichastny's dismissal and the appointment of Andropov to this sensitive and intensely unpopular position are interesting.

Semichastny was heartily disliked by Soviet intellectuals, particularly after his tirade against Boris Pasternak in 1958. At an ideological meeting following the publication of

Doctor Zhivago abroad, he had said of Pasternak, 'Even a pig does not shit where it eats' and had demanded that he be deported from the Soviet Union. After the Sinyavsky–Daniel trial he had asked the Party Presidium to sanction widescale arrests in order to eradicate ideological dissent. But this was not the reason for his dismissal. He was guilty of a major intelligence blunder – having failed to prevent the defection of Stalin's daughter, Svetlana Alliluyeva, he then proceeded to order Soviet secret agents in Europe to kidnap her and bring her back. This was clearly absurd, and showed that Semichastny knew very little about professional undercover work (until 1961 he had been head of the Komsomol). Although Alliluyeva's defection was a blow to the Stalinists, it was ridiculous to think of kidnapping her. For one thing, Stalin's daughter knew no state secrets, and, for another, she was not particularly important in her own right. The kidnap attempt exposed several key KGB agents in the West and they were subsequently arrested.

Although this happened in March 1967 (Alliluyeva had left the Soviet Union at the end of 1966 to attend the burial ceremony of her third husband, an Indian Communist), Semichastny was not dismissed immediately. The reason is probably that Suslov was also implicated in the affair, since it was he who had given permission for Alliluyeva to travel abroad. It was thus not in Suslov's interest that the two events – the defection and Semichastny's dismissal – be too closely connected. Moreover, Shelepin objected to the removal of Semichastny. But in May Shelepin underwent an emergency appendix operation. He was in hospital for eight days and while he was away the question of the leadership of the KGB was included in the normal Politburo agenda. Semichastny was not present at this meeting, which decided the whole matter in ten minutes, dismissing him and recommending Andropov as his successor. The actual appointment was made the following day by the Presidium of the Supreme Soviet. Brezhnev maintained his policy of offering a *nomenklatura* position (that is, one important enough to require recommendation from a high Party organ) to holders of office who had been dismissed and Semichastny was made Ninth Deputy Chairman of the Council of Ministers of the Ukrainian SSR, responsible for sport. Several new deputy chairmen of the KGB were appointed, including General Semyon Kuzmich Tsvigun, Brezhnev's relative by marriage (their wives were sisters) and his friend from the early post-war Dnepropetrovsk years, when Brezhnev was First Secretary of the obkom from 1945 to 1950 and Tsvigun worked in the same region. Tsvigun was appointed head of the newly created 'Fifth Chief Directorate' of the KGB, responsible for internal security. KGB involvement in internal affairs, including the supervision of intellectuals, police, nationalities, religion, etc., had been considered unsatisfactory under Semichastny and was now to be increased.

A month later Shelepin was transferred from his position as Central Committee Secretary responsible for the organs of control (the KGB, the police, the Committee of State and Party Control) to the chairmanship of the All-Union Central Council of Trade Unions. Viktor Grishin, the previous incumbent, had been promoted to be First Secretary of the Moscow city and regional Party committees. Shelepin was furious. When he arrived at his new large office in the Trade Union building, he found that it had a few special features, such as a door leading into a specially equipped massage parlour. He immediately had a solid wall built to replace the door, making sure at the same time that Grishin's taste for such esoteric office luxuries became widely known. But Brezhnev was tolerant in such matters as long as the offender was personally loyal to him. Some of the control functions which had been under Shelepin's supervision were now transferred to the KGB and Suslov took others over into his ideological department.

In 1969 Suslov made a last bid for the top Party position. Together with Mazurov and Shelepin, he prepared a letter which criticized Brezhnev's economic policy and tried to have it discussed at the spring Plenum of the Central Committee. When it was rejected by other members of the Politburo, Suslov realized that it could be used against him and withdrew it. From then on he became loyal to Brezhnev, accepting his role as 'second' secretary. The rule which called for the retirement of the upper echelons of the Party when they reached seventy years of age had already been forgotten, so that Suslov occupied his influential Politburo position for many years.

There were rumours that Andropov was very reluctant to accept the KGB position and had only taken it on under pressure and because of his simultaneous promotion within the Party hierarchy. He certainly was very ambitious at that time. He was much younger than the other Politburo members and he could see that men like Pyotr Shelest, Arvid Pel'she, G. I. Voronov and D. C. Polyansky had no future since they had already been promoted beyond their real abilities. The chairmanship of the KGB was not, however, considered to be a job from which the incumbent was likely to be promoted to Party leadership. To get on to the leadership track, Andropov needed to become a full member of the Politburo and to return to the Secretariat. With his experience as a diplomat and in the foreign department of the Central Committee he could have entertained hopes of becoming Foreign Minister, but Gromyko seemed to be in good health and was doing a good job. The best he could hope for was to secure Suslov's position, and Suslov's poor health (he suffered from diabetes) and advanced age seemed to make this the best bet. His tenure at the KGB would, perhaps, be very brief. As it turned out, Suslov lived to an advanced age without retiring and the Brezhnev era had only just begun. Andropov remained Chairman of the KGB for fifteen years, longer than any previous incumbent. He turned out to be the most successful, the most sophisticated and the most legalistic head in the history of that organization.

With the exception of Feliks Dzerzhinsky, the architect of

the security services who died from tuberculosis in 1926 at the age of forty-nine, the Soviet chiefs of security have all had short, stormy careers which have ended violently or in political disgrace. Vyacheslav Menzhinsky, who became head of the OGPU (or Chief Political Directorate, as the security services were then called) after Dzerzhinsky's death, died in 1934 in mysterious circumstances. Later it was rumoured that he had been murdered by Genrikh Yagoda, his successor. Under Menzhinsky the chief victims of the OGPU were the peasants. The forced collectivization of agriculture in 1929–32 was accompanied by mass repression, executions and deportations. Menzhinsky also assisted Stalin in organizing the first show trials of engineers and intellectuals in 1929–30, which resulted in many executions. When Yagoda took over the security services he organized the assassination of Sergei Kirov in 1934 and the subsequent mass repressions in Leningrad. He himself was arrested and executed in 1936. His successor, Nikolai Ezhov (Commissar of Internal Affairs when the OGPU was renamed the NKVD), was a sadist and mass executioner, the chief organizer of Stalin's Great Terror in 1936–38, during which many millions were executed or perished in the Arctic labour camps. Ezhov 'disappeared' in 1939, probably murdered. Lavrenti Beria, the new NKVD chief, proved to be more durable. He, too, was a sadist and mass murderer, but he created his own Georgian mafia which protected him while Stalin was alive. He became a full member of the Politburo and was responsible for the police and the labour camps as well as for security. He was also in charge of all secret research programmes, including the atom bomb project. He was arrested and shot after Stalin's death. V. N. Merkulov, who had been in charge of the Ministry of State Security before 1950, was also executed. Viktor Abakumov, who had succeeded Merkulov as head of the MGB and had been dismissed during the last few weeks of Stalin's life, was found guilty of mass repressions in Leningrad and executed in 1955. S. N. Kruglov took over the security system briefly in 1953, but he was dismissed in 1954 and later committed suicide when his actions during the war came under investigation.

When Stalin died, the security service was downgraded from a ministry to a State Committee, and an untimely death ceased to be the inevitable fate of the man in charge once he lost his position. Khrushchev's personal friend, General Ivan Serov, a professional security man, was appointed head of the KGB, but he, too, was abruptly dismissed in 1958 when it became too well known that he had been in charge of the brutal deportation of the Crimean Tartars and other North Caucasian nations in 1943–44. He was replaced by Shelepin until 1961, and then by Semichastny, both of them previously at the head of the Komsomol and without professional security experience. Both Shelepin and Semichastny ended their political lives in disgrace. Andropov is the only man who not only survived the job but also made himself more influential politically in the process. He also succeeded in making security work an acceptable background for a leader of the CPSU. Moreover, he became leader through a normal process of Party succession rather than through the long power struggle which many observers had predicted. It was his record as head of the KGB that made this possible.

Before Andropov's appointment it was customary for the chief of the security services to function not only as protector of the state and the Party but also as the personal henchman of the Party leader. He was a sword not merely in the hands of the Party, but in its leader's hands as well. Even in democratic states, the head of the security or intelligence system often reports directly and only to the Prime Minister rather than to parliament or the full cabinet, and indeed all security services (Western as well as Soviet) are sometimes called upon to act illegally, to perform what have now come to be called 'dirty tricks', which would normally be considered criminal operations. Although Andropov was aware that he too would have to carry out some measures which were outside the law, he was determined not to repeat the errors of his predecessors, who had been ready to take any action required of them by the Party leader.

Brezhnev would probably have preferred to increase his own personal power in 1967 by appointing someone from his own 'Dnepropetrovsk mafia' to the KGB position. He had managed to do this in 1966, when Nikolai Shchelokov, his old friend, was made Minister of Public Order (retitled Minister of Internal Affairs in 1969). Shchelokov had attended the same Metallurgical Institute in Dnepropetrovsk as Brezhnev in the early 1930s and was Vice-Chairman of the Moldavian government when Brezhnev was First Secretary of the Moldavian Central Committee. Later Shchelokov himself served as Secretary of the Moldavian Central Committee, until Brezhnev brought him to Moscow to be head of the Soviet police. He had no police experience and was not qualified for the position, but he was a Brezhnev man and this was important. Since the Brezhnev connection was his only qualification for the job he would clearly never be able to challenge Brezhnev's wishes. He could be counted upon to close his eyes to illicit acts or to cover up any accusations of corruption which might have a negative effect on Brezhnev's interests. It is more than likely that Brezhnev wanted this sort of person at the KGB as well, yet Andropov was not that kind of man. Although he enjoyed good relations with Brezhnev, he did not owe his position to him. He was probably a generally agreed upon choice, since Suslov, Shelepin and possibly even Kosygin were aware of the danger of having a KGB boss with no political clout and unlimited personal loyalty to the General Secretary. Brezhnev now had a man in charge of the KGB whose unquestioning obedience could not be taken for granted. The best he could do was to appoint Semyon Tsvigun and Viktor Chebrikov, both linked to him through Dnepropetrovsk, to be the two First Deputy Chairmen of the KGB. If Andropov gave up the KGB position within a few years, the next boss would be a Brezhnev man.

7

The KGB under Andropov

The structure, history and domestic and foreign functions of the KGB have been described in a number of books published in the West.[1] Most of the information comes from KGB defectors, from KGB agents who have been arrested abroad and from foreign intelligence. Something can also be gleaned from Soviet works on intelligence operations, including novels glorifying the work of Soviet agents. A great deal is known about Stalin's security system – it now forms part of every book on Soviet history written outside the Soviet bloc. It is not my intention to go over the same ground here. However, I shall say a little about what the KGB seemed like to a dissident, to a member of a movement with which the KGB had to deal as part of its complex task.

The Committee of State Security (KGB) was established by Khrushchev in 1954 from the remnants of Stalin's security system. It was to be a small organization and it was stripped of many of its previous functions. Khrushchev wanted to reduce the power of the secret police and to revive the ascendancy of the Party apparatus. During Stalin's time Party officials were even more in fear of the security system than ordinary citizens were. Under Khrushchev the prison camps (Gulag) were transferred to the Ministry of Public Order, although some prisons remained under KGB control. The KGB could no longer try cases. It could, however, make arrests (with the permission of the Procurator), detain people and investigate cases to prepare them for court proceedings.

In an understandable attempt to prevent the arbitrary arrests which were a feature of Stalin's rule, Khrushchev managed to create a system of legal double standards, one for Party members, the other for the rest of society. Political and ideological matters, particularly those which involved members of the Party, were removed from the jurisdiction of the KGB. The KGB could no longer arrest members of the Party, it could only present their cases for investigation. If investigation by the Party uncovered sufficient reason for a member to be expelled, only then could that person be arrested by the KGB or by the police. There were a number of occasions while Khrushchev was leader when a member of the Party was disciplined by the Party for actions which for ordinary people would have resulted in arrest and sentence to a prison labour camp. Such discipline took the form of an escalating series of reprimands: Party reprimand, strong Party reprimand, strong Party reprimand with warning and strong Party reprimand with warning and endorsement in the personal files.

Khrushchev also abolished the district (raion) units of the KGB, retaining larger regional (oblast) departments. This made thousands of KGB officials redundant and effectively reduced the number of secret informers, since they usually operated at a local, raion level. He introduced the position of 'Party informer' instead, operating from local Party Bureau level upwards and forming a pyramid of Party informers and investigators right up to the level of the Committee of Party and State Control of the Central Committee. An Ideological Commission was established to supervise ideological purity and prevent deviation. These measures considerably reduced the role played by the KGB in internal security. It acted only if there was suspicion of espionage, a leak of state secrets or a question of foreign connections. When Khrushchev initiated de-Stalinization drives which released those victims of the terror who were still alive, this exposed not only the scale of Stalin's crimes but also those who were responsible for the terror. People who returned from the labour camps exposed the investigators who had tortured them, the informers who had denounced them, the camp officials who had established brutal regimes. This rapidly eroded the credibility of the security organs, although as a rule no criminal charges were brought against security officials. The most notorious amongst them were usually transferred to civilian jobs or retired on pension. A radical overhaul of the system was too complex a task, particularly since many Party officials, including Khrushchev himself, were by no means innocent of the charge of having violated 'socialist principles of justice' in the past.

In 1958 Khrushchev attempted to renovate the KGB. In spite of his personal loyalty to Khrushchev, General Serov was dismissed and replaced by the First Secretary of the Komsomol, A. N. Shelepin, a careerist with immense political ambition. The Komsomol now took over the KGB internal network, replacing the cadres who had worked under Stalin and Beria. Local Komsomol secretaries were appointed as heads of local KGB offices and many professional Komsomol workers in Moscow took over the central departments of the KGB there. The result was that the professional level of KGB work deteriorated, although strict ideological vigilance was evident since Komsomol leaders were usually ideological dogmatists. Shelepin made a strong speech at the Twenty-Second Party Congress in 1961, disclosing some of Stalin's terrible crimes. After the Congress he was appointed head of the Committee of Party and State Control and a candidate member of the Party Presidium. Semichastny, the man who had replaced Shelepin as First Secretary of the Komsomol, now replaced him as head of the KGB. This was the organization which Andropov inherited in 1967.

As soon as Shelepin was moved over to the Trade Unions, Andropov transferred many functions of the Committee of Party and State Control and later the Ideological Commission to the KGB. The system of 'Party informers' was abolished and a network of secret, more professional informers began to develop. Andropov still kept the KGB well under Party control, but he clearly wanted to increase its influence and the power of its apparatus. He also wanted to make KGB officials more competent. He succeeded in both aims. The power of the KGB increased enormously and it began to be capable of acting not only against dissidents, Jewish activists and other forms of political opposition but also against Party officials and against corruption in the government system. The methods employed became more flexible and more sophisticated.

Under Andropov there was no place for Stalin's methods of arbitrary terror nor for the unprofessional clumsiness of the Sinyavsky–Daniel trial. The KGB began to be more careful in the preparation of cases, to plant evidence, to infiltrate dissident organizations and to use more technical methods of surveillance. In dealing with well-known dissidents, preference was shown for using pressure to encourage emigration; alternatively, instead of being brought to trial, people were forcibly deported or deprived of Soviet citizenship while they were abroad. Compared to Western standards of justice and fair judicial procedures, many of the trials seemed badly prepared. But by Soviet standards they appeared convincing, and they gave Andropov a favourable image as a defender of Party and state interests who, nonetheless, tried to preserve the norms of 'socialist legality'. The actions taken against dissidents might have given the KGB bad publicity abroad, but they had the reverse effect with the Communist Party and government structure, and this was more important to Andropov. He acquired the reputation within the Party of being a strong but just man, the guardian of the system. He, Suslov and Ustinov were the only Politburo members who were known to be modest in their personal life-style. Brezhnev and his 'team' from the Ukraine and Moldavia were known to enjoy luxurious country residences, hunting lodges, lavish parties, private cinemas and sometimes even those services which are called 'escort' services in the West.

Even before he moved to the KGB, Andropov was known to have close relations with certain literary and artistic figures. His daughter, Irina, married Aleksandr Filipov, an actor of the popular, avant-garde Tagansky theatre, and Andropov became friendly with Yuri Lyubimov, the director of this theatre and a brilliant innovator and performer. His relations with the theatre were discreet — there were constant problems with the Ministry of Culture and other ideological watchdogs, and he tried to protect Lyubimov. In fact, Andropov's literary connections were not without use for the KGB. By the 1970s a large part of the population no longer remembered the crimes of the Stalin era and the censors made sure that this remained a closed subject. A well-orchestrated campaign began in literature, the cinema and the theatre to improve the image of the security services. Thrillers reappeared as a popular genre, and films, plays and long television serials glorified the heroism of Soveit secret agents during the war and afterwards. Slowly the public attitude began to change. At the same time the KGB acted (often with success) against several corrupt officials. The general public was aware of the widespread official corruption, but in people's minds it was more closely associated with the party elite and even with the police (militia) than with the KGB. The KGB may have behaved badly in Czechoslovakia in 1968, but the general public in the Soviet Union knew little about that and cared even less. However it was a different story when the whole Party Presidium and the Government of the Azerbaijan Republic were dismissed for corruption, bribery and the embezzlement of public funds in 1969; this coup (the local KGB boss, Aliyev, was in charge of the clean-up operation) became the topic of many anecdotes and of local folklore.[2]

In 1970 Andropov found an opportunity to have the Secretary of the Leningrad obkom, Vasilii Tolstikov, dismissed. Tolstikov, who was well known as a playboy, had got drunk with a few girls on his pleasure boat and had accidentally crossed the border of the Soviet territorial waters not far from Leningrad. A border patrol boat arrested his craft and brought crew and passengers to the nearest border station for questioning. Tolstikov demanded that he be released instantly because of his political status, but he had no documents on him to prove who he was. When his identity was established, the officer in charge made a direct call to Andropov. Tolstikov was released, but in order to avoid a cover-up Andropov authorized an official commendation for the local border officer (border guards belong to the KGB) for his action. As a result the matter could not be ignored and Tolstikov was dismissed. Brezhnev, true to his policy of offering *nomenklatura* positions to disgraced officials, sent him to China as Soviet Ambassador, but in 1970, during the Cultural Revolution, the embassy job in China was tantamount to being sentenced to house arrest. Tolstikov's fate also passed into folklore.[3]

In the following year the notorious governing elite of Georgia, which operated like a mafia, was overthrown in a military-style operation. Georgia was legendary for corruption and black marketeering, and it was common knowledge that any car stolen in Moscow or Leningrad could be sold safely there, with no questions asked and no papers required. It was said that some local Georgian bosses organized an armed resistance to their overthrow, defending their houses which were like museums, filled with illicit treasure. Replacing the Georgian government was more difficult than the Azerbaijan operation, and the new Party leader, Shevarnadze, was under guard for several years and used bullet-proof cars because of several attempts on his life.

Details of these and other similar incidents became known, despite the silence of the Soviet press. It would seem that scandals of this magnitude are difficult to conceal. Foreign radio also played an important role in the dissemination of information. The KGB skilfully used foreign journalists, leaking essential items to them through KGB agents like the well-known Viktor Louis. Journalists friendly to the Soviet Union were appropriately rewarded:

they were the first to be told of important developments and were also given some stories which were not generally current. The foreign press was also used to disseminate the required image of the KGB leaders and the Party ideologues. But if previous KGB bosses sought to be known for their 'iron will' and 'uncompromising attitudes', for their 'true Bolshevik' or 'true Chekist' characters, the Andropov image as projected through a variety of channels was entirely different. After Brezhnev's death, when the Western media were combing their files to see what was known about Andropov, the papers and magazines were full of phrases such as the following: 'sophisticated', 'speaks English well', 'collects big-band records and relaxes with American novels', 'tolerates Hungarian-style goulash communism and economic decentralization', 'closet liberal', 'more pragmatic', 'open to political moderation and economic reform', 'possible new Kennedy', 'well-informed about foreign affairs', 'speaks little and to the point', 'known as a tough man to work for', 'is like Henry Kissinger', 'open-minded, westernized, master politician', 'has sought friendly discussions with dissident protesters', etc.[4] Many tabloids, of course, chose to describe him differently – Andropov was the 'butcher of Budapest', 'assassin of irritating dissidents', 'spymaster', 'inventor of psycho-prisons', 'expert on disinformation', etc.[5] Some journalists even professed to know which American books Andropov has on his shelf, demonstrating his strange attraction to Western culture. However, for any insider who knows a little about the current life-styles of Soviet leaders, all these signs of 'westernization' are meaningless. Brezhnev liked fast Western sports cars and smoked only American cigarettes; the ultra-conservative Pyotr Shelest imported Italian marble for his Crimean palace near Yalta. I doubt very much whether a single member of the Politburo has furnished his apartment or dacha with furniture made in Kaluga or Kalinin. They all have Japanese or German hi-fi systems and large collections of video films, records and foreign books, quite often from the stores of these items confiscated by customs officials from foreigners visiting the Soviet Union. The contents of Andropov's bookshelves therefore tell us little about the quality of the man.

As far as his success in changing KGB methods is concerned, the results have been mixed. It is true that the dissident (or democratic) movement has been effectively crushed and its leading figures are either in exile or prison or abroad in emigration. Andropov as General Secretary does not face any serious internal democratic opposition. But it took fifteen long years to do this job. And meanwhile many dozens of important books about Stalin's crimes, about *nomenklatura* corruption, about the failure of Khrushchev's economic reforms and about other problems have been written by dissident authors and published abroad in Russian or in foreign languages. Many novels which could never appear in the USSR have been published in other countries and smuggled back. The Jewish problem has attracted worldwide attention. However, about 260,000 Jews have been allowed to emigrate since 1971 and this new emigration (probably infiltrated by KGB agents) is very much involved in publicist activity in the West, critical of the Soviet Union: for example, in institutions like Radio Liberty, the Russian sections of the Voice of America, the BBC and Deutsche Welle, and on the editorial boards of Russian language newspapers and magazines abroad. In addition many émigrés work in academic centres for Soviet studies. Active dissident groups never consisted of more than a few hundred members, but they have gained publicity far out of proportion to their size. Anatolii Sharansky's case alone has attracted more Western attention than all Stalin's purges did in 1937.

I personally believe that this comparative leniency towards dissent created difficulties for Brezhnev but at the same time served to promote Andropov's advancement. Indeed, Andropov used the dissident problem for his own ends. His protracted cat-and-mouse tactics, in contrast to the terror used by Stalin's security men who arrested about 5,000 people daily in 1937 – in contrast even to Semichastny, who called, in 1966, for the rapid solution of the dissident problem by the arrest of 1,000 people – have paid dividends. The problem of dissent was exaggerated beyond its real proportions, which in turn made things more difficult for Brezhnev and his group as well as for local, often corrupt, Party officials. The persistent appearance of anti-Stalinist literature was used as a valid justification for the growth of the KGB apparatus and it kept the activities of the KGB in the headlines of the foreign press. In the Soviet political context, this publicity was good for the KGB. Even more interesting is the fact that amongst hundreds of *samizdat* books, memoirs, essays and articles, many of which have subsequently been published in the West, there is not a single work which has anything of substance to report about Andropov himself. There are criticisms and condemnations of Stalin's rule, criticisms of Lenin, Trotsky and other revolutionary leaders. There are many appalling stories about Ezhov, Yagoda, Beria, critical studies of Khrushchev, descriptions of Molotov, Malenkov, Kaganovich, and even Suslov. Both the previous and the present prison camps and prisons are described. There are ironic works dealing with Brezhnev and the 'Brezhnev mafia', and many stories, some apocryphal and some documented, about corrupt Party officials and government ministers under him. All these works seriously erode the prestige of the Party leadership of Brezhnev and his predecessors. There are, of course, many works which criticize the KGB, but I do not know of a single one which blames Andropov personally. After fifteen years of heading the KGB, nobody can prove his personal responsibility for excesses in the activities of the security organs. Suggestions can be made, but there is no hard evidence.

Perhaps even more surprising is the fact that, as Mark Frankland reported recently from Moscow, 'part at least of the intelligentsia has great hopes of the Andropov era'.[6] (This is not true, though, of the ordinary man in the street, in Moscow or in the provinces, who knows nothing of Andropov's 'liberalism' and views his KGB background with some apprehension.) After eighteen years of Brezhnev's indulgent rule, with the KGB poised against all dissent, the last thing which Soviet intellectuals desired was the rise of Konstantin Chernenko, the most loyal of the 'Brezhnevites', a person with no record of repression, clearly not a 'strong man', and almost certainly a supporter of 'collective leadership'. This is an interesting political and social phenomenon. I am sure that if an American-style election had been held in the Soviet Union after Brezhnev's death with Chernenko and Andropov as the two main contenders, Andropov would have won on the promise to fight corruption and put the 'house in order'. However, under the Soviet system of leadership both remained relatively unknown figures to the general public.

The KGB worked hard to discredit the dissident movement in the USSR. But it worked even harder to discredit the 'Brezhnev mafia' and to clear the way for the 'Andropov era'.

8

The KGB against Dissent

Political dissent has not been tolerated in the Soviet Union since the time of Lenin. This is typical of a one-party state, and is even more typical of a one-party Communist state. According to Communist doctrine Communist society represents the highest form of social development and the only possible 'just' society and therefore any expression of anti-socialism or anti-Communism is treated as a crime. This fact was copiously reflected in Stalin's Criminal Code, which included many complex definitions of political crimes, anti-Soviet activity, anti-socialist views, etc., and which made it possible for people to be arrested and imprisoned for any anti-socialist or critical opinions even if these were never expressed in public but only in private. In the 1930s the search for the enemies of socialism reached a state of general paranoia.

It is to Khrushchev's credit that he put an end to this paranoid attitude towards criticism. By denouncing Stalin's crimes, and by rehabilitating many of his victims and adopting other practical measures, he brought about a change in the meaning of the term 'political crime'. This does not mean that the Soviet Union became a country in which a pluralism of ideas was allowed, or where there was democratic tolerance. Nonetheless, the scope of permitted criticism was increased enormously. In the Stalin era it was inadmissible to criticize economic inefficiency or the poor quality of Soviet consumer goods or industrial machinery.

Praise for the technical superiority of German planes or American cars could incur a criminal charge. Under Khrushchev, however, people were free to complain of incompetence in the work of ministries, factories or plants. They could compare Soviet goods and equipment unfavourably with foreign products, and they could refer to the positive achievements of the American economy, particularly with regard to agriculture. By Soviet standards this represented tremendous political evolution. Apart from personal criticism, which, not surprisingly, was not appreciated by the Soviet leaders, anti-Soviet views were considered criminal only if expressed in public. Anything that was said privately, in the family circle or amongst friends, did not constitute a crime.

The result of this relaxation, however minimal it might seem in the West, was that under Khrushchev political dissent became possible. In the new Criminal Code, adopted in 1960 and still in force (with some amendments), only one article incorporated the principle of a punishable political crime. This was Article 70, dealing with 'Anti-Soviet agitation and propaganda', which made slander of the Soviet political system or the distribution, preparation or accumulation of anti-Soviet literature punishable by deprivation of freedom for a period of from six months to seven years if it was carried out with the purpose of weakening or undermining Soviet power or engaging in dangerous crimes against the state.[1] This article is, of course, open to criticism from a legal point of view – in particular one can find fault with official Soviet judicial commentaries on it. However it was much milder than Stalin's draconian laws. It could not be automatically assumed that the author of a sharply critical book or essay *intended* to weaken or undermine Soviet power: authors could argue, in fact, that their criticism was intended to improve the socialist system and to strengthen Soviet authority. In any case, the discussion of 'democratic socialism' or 'socialism with a human face' violated neither the letter nor the spirit of the law. The weakness of Article

70 as an instrument against political dissent became clear during the debates provoked by the Sinyavsky–Daniel trial and in the speeches made by the defence lawyers.[2] To correct this state of affairs, the KGB under Semichastny sponsored a law in 1966 (adopted by the Supreme Soviet as an amendment to Article 190 of the Criminal Code), Article 190–1: 'The distribution of false information which slanders the Soviet state and social system'. Although this law imposes milder penalties than Article 70, its language is general and imprecise, and therefore more useful to the authorities. It stipulates that the distribution in *verbal* (*oral*) form of false information about the Soviet state and social system or the distribution of this information in *handwritten, printed or any other form* is punishable by deprivation of freedom for a period of up to three years (or exile for up to five years).

The fact that anti-Soviet utterances would no longer be tolerated, and that the *intention* of weakening or undermining Soviet power was no longer relevant in establishing guilt, made this law a far stronger weapon against dissent. Virtually all means of communication – oral statements, letters, tape-recordings, etc. – would now be treated in the same way as written works. The only possible defence for dissident authors and activists was to be sure of their information, to be scrupulous in their use of facts. Any general criticism of the Soviet system or of Communist ideology could be treated as a criminal offence. Article 190–1 did not put an end to dissent. On the contrary, it had the effect of making dissent more efficient, by making it concentrate on facts, figures, and verifiable information, rather than on rumour or generalities. Thus Andrei Amalrik's well-known *Will the Soviet Union Survive until 1984?*,[3] a speculative work, full of generalizations with little factual analysis, was condemned as anti-Soviet and Amalrik was tried and sentenced. At the same time the *samizdat* journal, *The Chronicle of Current Events*, which listed well-documented abuses of human rights, arrests, dismissals and the repression of religious and national groups, without editorial comment, survived for many years.[4] It did not contain any inaccurate information, and this was the main strength of the type of *samizdat* it represented. Later some false information was planted in it – information from the provinces is difficult to verify – and the *Chronicle* too became a candidate for repression.

When the human rights movement began to develop after 1966, the decision was made to work within the limits of Soviet legality and to criticize the regime with facts rather than with general pamphlets. Although some polemical works continued to appear, they were often written and published abroad and smuggled back into the Soviet Union. Some of them seemed to be the work of provocateurs.

Since there is no distinction in Soviet law between common crimes and political crimes, and there is only one Criminal Code, theoretically at least, the ordinary police have the power to deal with all violations of the law, including those covered by Articles 70 and 190–1. All crimes (excluding those committed by members of the armed forces or those involving espionage, which are dealt with in closed court) are investigated and then considered by the ordinary courts. Nonetheless, it became customary for the KGB to make arrests and carry out investigations of charges made on the basis of Articles 70 and 190–1. When the majority of the dissident groups began to restrict their activity to legal methods, it seemed, at first, as if the KGB would have difficulty in stemming the flow of dissent. In the period 1967–71 the amount of *samizdat* literature of various kinds, much of it published abroad and all of it highly critical, actually increased rapidly. Although there were many arrests on political charges during this period, the trend continued. Each political trial turned into a debate in which the KGB investigators tried to show that the accused were spreading false, slanderous information, while the defendants and their witnesses insisted that their criticism was justified and based on ascertainable facts and events. Although most of the defendants were found guilty and sentenced to periods of imprisonment or exile, the moral victory went to the accused, not to the KGB.

It is difficult to say what it was exactly that made the Party bureaucracy and the KGB change tactics without changing the law. It is probable that in 1970 the Politburo discussed the problem of political dissent (or as they would have phrased it, 'political subversion organized by foreign intelligence centres') and issued new directives calling for more decisive measures. It was, of course, the KGB and Party organizations which were to carry out these new measures. In the course of the next decade, political dissent was systematically and methodically eliminated, which earned for the KGB a great deal of adverse publicity abroad and also the hatred of the Soviet intelligentsia. There has been a clear tendency in the West to single out the KGB for blame, while taking a more positive view of Brezhnev and his policy of détente and rapprochement. Within the Soviet Union, however, in the absence of any indication to the contrary, it was realized that the KGB would not be acting independently of the Party apparatus. At a local level, indeed, it was quite often Party officials who demanded action from the KGB and the police. It would be quite wrong to imagine that Brezhnev was ready to permit dissent while Andropov was not. The Party leaders were no more tolerant of dissent than the KGB, but it was the job of the KGB to eliminate it.

By 1969–70 it was already clear that the normal processes of justice were too inefficient and time-consuming for the fight against dissent. Each trial was a painful experience for the KGB. The preparatory investigations could last many months, and the trials themselves attracted a great deal of attention and publicity, giving the defendants the opportunity of expressing their views and of entering into a limited form of dialogue with officials. After the trial the accused, particularly if found guilty, became an international celebrity while the KGB and the Soviet regime were again subjected to worldwide criticism and condemnation. Political repression clearly required a special system of 'justice', like the Cheka or Stalin's secret 'troika' courts, which could do its work outside the glare of world publicity. But it was impossible to revive old methods, and in any case no-one was prepared to do this. Innovation was required. To what extent credit should be given to Andropov personally for devising new methods is difficult to say. Perhaps it is unimportant – the KGB as a whole was responsible for the elimination of dissent.

One of the methods used extensively against dissidents in the decade 1970–80 which has been widely discussed in the West is their commitment to mental hospitals. In part this was an attempt to discredit dissent both within the Soviet Union and abroad as some form of psychological abnormality. It was also a convenient way out in cases where a trial presented serious difficulties due to lack of evidence or the prospect of a forceful and well-argued defence. In fact, this method of dealing with dissent backfired rather badly – international opinion considered incarceration in a mental hospital to be more cruel than imprisonment or exile. Amnesty International classed it with torture. By the end of the 1970s well-known dissidents seldom wound up in forensic mental hospitals, although psychiatric 'treatment' was still being widely used in the provinces to deal with less prominent figures. There were, at the same time, cases of dissidents who did, in fact, have a history of psychiatric problems, which complicated the task of the World Psychiatric Association in its attempts to monitor the abuse of psychiatry in the Soviet Union. (On 9 February 1983 the Soviet Society of Psychiatrists and Neurologists resigned from the World Psychiatric Association in order to forestall a public debate on the expected British motion from the Royal College of Psychiatry to expel the Soviet group, because of the imprisonment of dissidents in psychiatric hospitals.)

Extensive use has also been made of emigration as a means of getting rid of active dissidents. Jewish and German emigration became a mass phenomenon in 1971, and since then about 250,000 Jews and 80,000 Volga Germans have left the Soviet Union. A number of political critics were given the choice of either being charged and tried or applying for permission to emigrate, whether or not they were Jews. Many chose emigration. Others began by refusing to leave, but after a three-, five-, or even seven-year spell in the labour camps, prison or exile and the threat of a second charge upon release (since most continued their political activity), they often changed their minds. Hundreds of members of various human rights groups and dissident literary and scientific figures are now living in the West. This method of dealing with dissidents not only cleared the Soviet Union of active dissent – it also gave the KGB excellent opportunities of infiltrating various émigré organizations, anti-Soviet propaganda centres and academic institutions. Although the KGB has used both the Jewish emigration and the Volga-German emigration for purposes of infiltration, it is easy to exaggerate the danger this presents. It is unfortunately the case that within the émigré communities in Israel, Paris, Munich and New York, and in the Russian language émigré press, accusations and counter-accusations of being connected with the KGB are rife, which creates a strange and tense atmosphere in those communities and organizations which employ a number of former Soviet citizens.

In the last decade the KGB has become much more adept in the technique of deliberately planting material, launching it into *samizdat* circulation and then using it to bring charges under Articles 70 or 190–1 if the bait is taken by a human rights group. Checking the accuracy of information is extremely difficult in the Soviet Union. For example, a local source may report the names of political prisoners who in fact turn out to be people who have been imprisoned for common crimes like burglary or rape; the central human rights groups have no way of examining the particulars of each case. Similarly, the names of people who are genuinely ill can easily be planted in the lists compiled for campaigns of protest against the abuse of psychiatry. False reports of strikes, protests by national minorities, etc. have turned up in the appeals of Moscow human rights groups and Helsinki monitoring groups, and in various publications. It is difficult, later, to find out who was responsible for this 'deliberately false information', and in the 1970s such methods were often used to bring charges against Moscow or Kiev groups who trusted their provincial sources.

Dissidents were also put under pressure at work. The KGB, in close collaboration with the Party organization and administrative personnel at places of employment, provided compromising information with the result that dissidents were demoted, dismissed, expelled from the Party, blocked in promotion or prevented from gaining higher academic degrees or from publishing their work. These restrictions are covered by the general term "harassment". Measures such as these proved particularly effective against intellectuals who were not yet openly involved in any form of active political opposition but who supported dissidents financially or read *samizdat* or protest works smuggled in from abroad. During pre-trial investigations or before making an arrest, the KGB or police usually search the suspect's apartment and remove manuscripts, books and private letters which are considered to be anti-Soviet. Lists of what was taken are often published by dissidents themselves, to show the type of literature that is of interest to the police. During the pre-trial investigation and lengthy interrogation the KGB makes a great effort to discover the source of forbidden books or manuscripts as well as the names of other readers. When the arrested person co-operates with the KGB, dozens of people can be named. For instance, in 1973, in the notorious case of Pyotr Yakir and Viktor Krasin, who actively collaborated with the KGB and later held a press conference for foreign journalists, more than a hundred names of assistants, sources and sympathizers were disclosed. Three or four of these people were later arrested. The rest were treated more leniently, merely being warned, dismissed from their jobs or demoted, or expelled from the Party. These methods usually suffice to prevent further sympathy for active dissidents, particularly when people implicated by a confession feel that they have been betrayed.

The KGB also provides the administration of research institutes and universities and the directors and Party secretaries of factories, departments, ministries and other state organizations with lists of those who have signed petitions or letters of protest. It supplies information about the political activities of people outside their normal working hours, often accompanying this information with recommendations for suitable retribution. Occasionally the result will be the quiet dismissal of the person thus implicated. More often the KGB report will be read out in public at a meeting called at the place of employment to criticize the person concerned and decide on his or her future. There have been several cases in Moscow, Novosibirsk and Leningrad where scientists have been demoted, dismissed or even stripped of their academic degrees as a result of this kind of 'gentle' KGB treatment.

It is more difficult to link the use of blackmail and intimidation directly to the KGB. Complaints about KGB involvement in techniques such as these are generally dismissed out of hand. The blackmail attempt is usually made by post, through letters to the dissident and sometimes to his or her friends as well, or by telephone. The disclosure is threatened of some unpleasant fact like an extra-marital relationship, sexual aberration, past criminal activity or collaboration with the NKVD (some people who were imprisoned in Stalinist labour camps acted as informers then in order to survive) unless the person threatened desists from dissident activity. Quite often the blackmail is effective, inducing depression and silence.

One of the ways in which the KGB has been able to compromise organized groups is through the use of infiltrators and provocateurs. In all the recent trials of human rights groups, Helsinki monitors and Jewish activists, members of the group have appeared as witnesses for the prosecution. KGB informers are easy to recruit in the camps by offering, as a reward, a reduction of sentence. The infiltration of dissident groups not only makes subsequent trials easier to organize by ensuring proper witnesses, it is also an effective way of discrediting the groups in the eyes of the Soviet public. The best-known example of this kind was the role played by the KGB provocateur Semyon Lipavsky in the case of Anatolii Sharansky, which was widely discussed in the international press in 1978. Lipavsky attracted a great deal of attention because he was also a temporary CIA agent. President Carter made a special statement about him at a press conference on 15 June 1977, categorically denying the charges that he had been connected with the CIA. However, Lipavsky had already held a press conference of his own, 'How the CIA recruited me',[5] in which he revealed details of his work as a double agent.

The KGB has become much more skilled in the preparation of cases – much has been learnt since the notorious Sinyavsky–Daniel trial of 1966. In Great Britain or the USA such trials would hardly result in conviction, for a moderately intelligent defence lawyer could quickly demolish the prosecution's 'evidence'. But in the Soviet Union a defence lawyer has no independent power to call witnesses or to conduct investigations. Even his right to cross-examine is limited. Defendants have a restricted choice of defence lawyers, and in any case all lawyers who are permitted to appear in court are state employees. In the Sinyavsky–Daniel trial, the lawyer was a man of integrity and presented a formidable defence, but he was disqualified soon afterwards and lost permission to appear in court. These rules of judicial procedure and restrictions on the defence were not invented in the Brezhnev era – they were introduced by Khrushchev along with the new Criminal and Civil Codes of 1960. They represented an improvement over the secret trials of Stalin's time, when no defence at all was possible, but Khrushchev never intended to create a genuinely liberal judicial system. He wanted the Party to control everything, including the courts.

The KGB's most favoured method for dealing with prominent dissidents, the celebrities of the Western media such as Alexander Solzhenitsyn, Mstislav Rostropovich, Lev Kopelev, Viktor Nekrasov, Pyotr Grigorenko, Vladimir Maximov, Vasilii Aksenov, Valerii Chalidze and Aleksandr Ginzburg, was to deprive them of citizenship during trips abroad, to deport them or to exchange them for imprisoned Soviet spies or Communist leaders, as in the case of the exchange of Vladimir Bukovsky for the leader of the Chilean Communist Party, Luis Corvalan, in 1976. As a rule this treatment was reserved for people who had already achieved a high degree of professional recognition before openly challenging the regime. In such cases a criminal trial would stir up too much publicity and would be unpopular within the Soviet Union as well as abroad. The exile of dissidents is not considered to be an excessively severe penalty in the West but is often thought to indicate a more humane and flexible attitude. It is likely that Andrei Sakharov would have been sent abroad rather than to Gorky had he not been a nuclear physicist who had previously been involved in the H-bomb project.

Other new tactics adopted by the KGB included drafting dissidents into the army, blocking university entrance, arranging post-educational appointments to very distant parts of the country and blacklisting for foreign trips. Some of these measures had the reverse effect to that intended, for instead of suppressing moderate dissent they provoked open, active opposition. In general, however, the dissident movement as an active force is now very weak. There are, of course, many newcomers, but they tend to be young and inexperienced, unlike the prominent scientists, academics, musicians, writers, journalists, actors, old Bolsheviks and sometimes even members of the establishment who were at the centre of the movement in the 1960s and early 1970s. It is much easier for the authorities to deal with these new recruits.

In response to the repression of 'law-abiding' dissent, new

underground groups with various programmes have started
to appear since the late 1970s. They use clandestine, con-
spiratorial methods and there have even been a few cases of
terrorism, such as the bomb explosion in the Moscow
Metro in 1977. Although it took a year to find and arrest the
few members of the Armenian group who planted the
bomb, the power of the KGB is such that the survival and
expansion of these underground groups is unlikely.

It is clear that Andropov, as head of the KGB, has played a
major role in the programme to eliminate political dissent.
Although there is no record of his personal participation in
particular cases, it is not entirely true that Andropov, as
Peter Wilsher, foreign editor of *The Sunday Times*,
maintains,

> . . . by a striking sleight-of-hand, has distanced himself from
> all this, giving the impression – quite falsely – that all he is
> interested in is the higher reaches of foreign policy and
> ideological rectitude.
>
> To a large extent Andropov's trick has worked. He hardly
> rates a mention in Amnesty International's roll-call of
> human rights villains. Instead, he has diverted attention to
> his public utterances – he has three times been asked to
> deliver the prestigious annual Lenin Memorial address,
> most recently in the spring of this year.[6]

There have been a number of occasions when senior KGB
officials have clearly stated their intention to eradicate dissent in the Soviet Union. Brezhnev and other political leaders
described political dissidents as 'accomplices, if not actual
agents, of imperialism'.[7] It would be unnatural for the KGB
chairman to distance himself from this campaign even when
speaking about political problems. His audience would expect him to report on problems of security as well. It is true
that in 1981 and 1982 Andropov did not touch on the topic
of dissent. But in previous years, and especially during President Carter's crusade for human rights, his views were
expressed quite clearly, sometimes even cynically. In a long
speech made at a special meeting of Soviet and KGB officials

to celebrate the 100th anniversary of the birth of Feliks Dzerzhinsky, Andropov, more explicitly than any other Party leader, tried to link all forms of political dissent with the 'special services of imperialism'.

> This is why Western propaganda makes so much fuss about 'human rights' and about the so-called 'dissidents' . . . Soviet citizens have the right to criticize and to make proposals. This right is guaranteed by Article 49 of the Constitution, which forbids repression for criticism . . . But it is an entirely different matter when a few individuals transform criticism into anti-Soviet activity, violate the law, supply Western propaganda centres with false information, disseminate false rumours, try to organise anti-social actions . . . These renegades have no support from the Soviet people. This is why they never try to make open speeches in factories or on collective farms or in other state organizations. They know very well that they would be thrown out of such meetings . . . The existence of dissidents in the Soviet Union is only possible because of publicity campaigns in the foreign press, and support for them through diplomatic, secret and other special services who pay 'dissidents' generously in foreign currency and by other means. There is no difference between the payment which secret services make to their own agents and to dissidents . . .[8]

There are many elements of demagoguery in this long speech, of which the above is merely a short extract. Andropov is well aware of the fact that many dissidents would be delighted to have the opportunity to express their views and criticisms publicly at meetings of workers or peasants. The Party and the KGB have never afforded them the opportunity. Even silent peaceful gatherings of dissidents on Pushkin Square in Moscow on Constitution Day are immediately dispersed by the police and by activists working with the police. Political dissidents are not given the chance to express their views in the Soviet press – KGB censorship prevents this. And if they publish their own leaflets, they are immediately liable to arrest.

In other parts of this speech, Andropov accepts that not all dissidents are the paid agents of imperialism. There are some

> . . . who do not understand the real truth. These people are given advice and explanations to help them to understand reality. If they persist in their actions and continue to be so-called 'dissidents' and even violate the law, we treat them quite differently. There are, unfortunately, a few people like this in our society, just as there are thieves, speculators, those who take bribes and other common criminals. The former (dissidents) and the latter groups damage our society and we treat them accordingly. They must be punished with the full force of Soviet law . . . By the way, it must be said that the number of people who are now sentenced for anti-Soviet activity is much lower than in previous periods of Soviet history. There are just a few . . . This is the real picture of the so-called problem of 'dissent'.[9]

It is unnecessary to point out that this picture is very far from true. If Andropov seriously believed that the Soviet system was so perfect that there were no social or political grounds for serious dissent, why, in his long speech about the glorious history of the Soviet *Chekists*, established by 'The Knight of the Revolution' Feliks Dzerzhinsky, did he say nothing about the various security chiefs who operated in the gap between Dzerzhinsky's death in 1926 and his own accession as the man in charge of the modern 'Cheka'? (There were actually *eleven* successors to Dzerzhinsky before his own arrival on the scene.) Only four lines of his speech contain a vague reference to the fact that

> . . . there were individual years which were darkened by illegal repressions, violations of the principles of socialist legality, and of Lenin's norms of party and state life . . . Our party decisively eliminated these violations and created the strong foundations of strict socialist legality.[10]

This is his only reference to a period which lasted twenty-six years and is actually the main source of modern dissent. At least half of all *samizdat* works circulating in the Soviet Union at present are concerned with violations of the 'norms of socialist legality' during the long era of Stalin's tyranny. Although Andropov showed himself to be well informed about Western publicity for Soviet dissidents, he also knows quite well that many of the methods used against them (and only partly detailed above) are illegal and violate the principles of socialist legality. It is not yet a question of terror in the historic, Stalinist sense, but it is possible to speak of 'moral and economic terror', a comprehensive system of depriving active dissidents of almost everything of value: education, employment, academic and research facilities, press or other media sources, income, and, if they still do not behave, freedom as well.

The KGB is also responsible for dealing with problems of dissent among the national minorities. This is usually the task of its Republican departments. From the memoirs of Grigorenko it is known that in 1967–68 Andropov had personal responsibility for the thorny problem of the Crimean Tartars, who had been deported from the Crimea to Uzbekistan in 1944 and were fully rehabilitated as a nation only in 1967. There were about half a million Tartars in 1967 and many of them wanted to return to their historic homeland after rehabilitation. However the official policy was to allow them to live anywhere *except* in the Crimea. Grigorenko, who was actively involved in their affairs, describes a meeting between Tartar representatives and Andropov's team at the beginning of 1968:

> The last time a delegation was received was in connection with the decree of the Presidium of the Supreme Soviet of September 5, 1967. This was the most false, the most hypocritical decree of all those issued in respect to these people. It began with a declaration that the Crimean Tatars had been charged with treason to the motherland and that there was no basis on which this charge would be annulled. But the annullment *was* justified by the fact that a new generation that had never known the war had come of age.

The greatest treachery of all was that by this decree the Crimean Tatars were deprived of the right to their own nationality. They were referred to as 'citizens of Tatar nationality who had previously lived in the Crimea.'

This decree of political rehabilitation made the exile of the Crimean Tatars from the Crimea permanent. The second part of the decree said that citizens of Tatar nationality who had previously lived in the Crimea were permitted to reside *throughout the entire territory of* the Soviet Union, *taking into account passport regulations.* And when these passport regulations were later determined, it was written that Crimean Tatars were not permitted to settle in the Crimea. In connection with the decree, the Crimean Tatars demanded a meeting with representatives of the Politburo. The meeting actually took place. The Politburo sent a group headed by Andropov and consisting of the Prosecutor General Rudenko and the Minister of Internal Affairs, Shcholokov — all representatives of organs of police repression. The fourth member of the commission was the secretary of the Presidium of the Supreme Soviet, Georgadze.

When the meeting had convened and Andropov had started to speak, a Crimean Tatar rose and asked, 'Comrade Andropov, are you here as a candidate member of the Politburo or as chairman of the KGB?'

'What's the difference?' Andropov laughed.

'There is a difference,' said the Crimean Tatar. 'If you are here as the chairman of the KGB, we will leave.'

'It is obvious that I am here on the instructions of the Politburo and in its name.'

Conversation throughout the meeting was hypocritical. Andropov and Shcholokov declared that the passport rules had no practical significance. To the question of why there was no such rule for Russians and Ukrainians, they did not give a coherent reply. The representatives of the Crimean Tatars asked whether they could call people to assembly in their respective districts in order to tell them about the talks.

'Yes, certainly,' said Andropov. 'I will see that instructions are issued to provide you with the necessary halls and not to hinder the conduct of the meetings.'

This was a lie. The local authorities received instructions

that they were forbidden to permit the Crimean Tatars to carry out their meetings. When the Crimeans requested to have their meetings and referred to Andropov, the authorities declined to reply.[11]

For Andropov all these unpleasant years in the KGB are now past history. Perhaps those fifteen years of security work did not show us the 'real Andropov', yet he can hardly be totally absolved of blame. However, he was not the only person responsible for the harsh treatment of dissidents. Brezhnev and his 'mafia' were ultimately responsible for domestic affairs during that period of Soviet history which will be called the 'Brezhnev era'. I tend to agree with Professor Stephen Cohen in his assessment of Andropov's future.

> . . . Andropov seems to have been the most reform-minded senior member of Brezhnev's Politburo, an impression he chose to reinforce cautiously in his first policy speech as the new General Secretary. Nor does his 15 years as head of the KGB disqualify him as a pote1tial reformer. Indeed, Andropov may be the only current leader who can assuage conservative fear of reform. And lest we forget that politicians sometimes rise above their former careers, Khrushchev once was called '*the butcher* of the Ukraine' for his part in Stalin's terror.[12]

9

The KGB against Brezhnev

Brezhnev was popular within the Party elite because of his principle that the holders of important state and Party positions should enjoy a reasonable stability and security of tenure. He was not an impulsive man; he was not particularly bright but neither was he stupid. He never aspired to be a superior, god-like figure in the manner of Stalin. Khrushchev often treated his Politburo colleagues with undisguised contempt and considered them no more than dutiful orderlies. When they did something he disapproved of he would raise his voice and swear at them – boorish behaviour which was quite typical for Party leaders of the Stalin generation. Brezhnev was quiet and tolerant, considered to be a good comrade, well-disposed towards his colleagues. When he was forced to make changes in the Politburo for any reason he used to give those who were dismissed high *nomenklatura* posts, so that they could maintain their comfortable life-styles. He gave Party officials the maximum security of tenure, while Soviet and state officials were treated as civil servants, not as elected politicians answerable to their constituencies.

This policy of 'stability' was not without its problems. Younger Party or state officials had to wait for promotion while the whole establishment grew older and older. Vacancies occurred only when someone died or became too ill to continue working and often even in these cases deputies of the former incumbents, old men themselves, were waiting to fill the vacancy. Perhaps the replacement of the ailing Kosygin, aged seventy-six, by the seventy-five-year-old Tikhonov is the best example of the phenomenon. Death from old age while still in office became the norm. Robert Daniels has estimated that of the 319 Central Committee members elected in 1981 at the Twenty-Sixth Party Congress, 95 were already members or candidate members of the Central Committee in 1961, and 55 became members at the Twenty-Third Party Congress in 1966.[1] If one takes into account the fact that forty to fifty members of the Central Committee are on a 'rotation list' because they are ordinary workers, *kolkhozniks*, scientists, writers or other representatives of 'the people', the stability of professional Party workers becomes very obvious.

There has been much criticism in the West of the old age of Soviet leaders: they have been called a 'gerontocracy' and reference made to the 'sclerotic leadership', etc. But in fact the durability of the Soviet leaders was considered to be part of their legitimacy, and the situation suited the Western powers. Foreign governments were quite happy to deal with a predictable (and inefficient) Politburo and were not really looking forward to change. Both Henry Kissinger and Alexander Haig expected trouble from the younger men who would inevitably come to power in the Kremlin. This is reflected in the unusual editorial article in *The Times* of 20 December 1979 which congratulated Brezhnev on his seventy-third birthday and praised his style – in particular the caution he showed in only using Soviet power

> . . . in situations where there was little or no risk of a direct confrontation with the United States. It has even been withdrawn when not wanted, as it was from Egypt. Such prudence and realism in the pursuit of advantage is what the West has learned to respect.

The Times was less optimistic about his successors:

> The worry is that his successors could be less prudent. Unscarred by memories of the war, inexperienced in diplomacy, fascinated by the power at their disposal and possibly

without the teams of westernized advisers which Mr Brezhnev
has sensibly built up, they could miscalculate.

It was, of course, ironic, that a few days after this editorial
appeared Brezhnev launched his military occupation of
Afghanistan, an operation which carried great risk and was
based on many miscalculations.

The 'stability' of the top leadership had a further negative
effect. In conditions of the absence of freedom of the press,
the impossibility of investigative journalism and the immunity
of Party officials from the police and KGB investigation, it
led to an extensive growth of official corruption at every
level. Party discipline diminished, nepotism became a common phenomenon and the ideological and administrative
prestige of the Party was on the decline. It was this corruption within the Party which finally enabled Andropov to
become Brezhnev's successor.

After the Twenty-Third Party Congress, Brezhnev formed
his own eleven-member Politburo, including, besides himself, Voronov, Kirilenko, Kosygin, Mazurov, Pel'she,
Podgorny, Polyansky, Shelest, and his rivals Suslov and
Shelepin. The only member who was really a Brezhnev man
was Kirilenko, who was entrusted with chairing meetings of
the Secretariat and the Politburo when Brezhnev was absent.
The most likely successors to Brezhnev, if he were to die,
were considered to be Kirilenko, and, with some reservations, Suslov, while Shelepin, his arch rival, would certainly
take the opportunity if it presented itself. Gradually Brezhnev
managed both to change the composition of the Politburo
and to enlarge it to fourteen members. Mazurov, Shelest,
Voronov, Polyansky, Shelepin and Podgorny were dismissed
or transferred to less prominent positions. New members
like Kunaev, Tikhonov, Grechko, Shcherbitsky and
Chernenko were old friends of Brezhnev. Andropov's
chances for the top job in this Politburo were very small.
When speculation began about the Kremlin succession after
Brezhnev's stroke in 1975, and later in 1978–79 when it

was obvious that he was unwell, Andropov's name was occasionally mentioned, but Kirilenko and the newcomer Chernenko continued to be the favourites of the foreign press.

It was, ironically enough, President Carter with his human rights policy who enhanced Andropov's power in the Politburo and increased his chances of inheriting Brezhnev's mantle. Carter over-reacted to the arrest of human rights activists in Moscow by making the fate of Orlov, Ginzburg and Sharansky the cornerstone of American–Soviet relations. He was probably sincere in thinking that he was making demands on Brezhnev and Kosygin, but he was, in fact, behaving as if Brezhnev had the same dictatorial power that Stalin had possessed. The Party had charged the KGB with the task of ridding the country of dissidents, and this meant that the arrests and impending trials were entirely within the competence of the KGB. Brezhnev's détente policy and his reputation thus became hostage to the fate of a few dissidents, and their fate in turn depended on the KGB and on Andropov, who thus became a linchpin in decisions of foreign policy and the real arbiter of the East–West dialogue. Whatever his feelings might have been then about the necessity for détente, he was already contending for Brezhnev's position and was therefore unlikely to do anything that would enhance the prestige of Brezhnev or of his faction.

The trials of dissidents produced a great deal of unfavourable international publicity for the Soviet Union. I came across only one Western newspaper during that period which understood that they were designed to demonstrate that Andropov, 'more than others, is now deciding policy'.[2]

Andropov's ambitions for the top job were already apparent and by 1977–78 his chances were very strong. Brezhnev was ailing and unable to take an active part in all the affairs of state and Party. His resignation would clearly have been in the national interest but his immediate circle, and in particular Chernenko, wanted him to retain his position for a while. Chernenko understood that while he and Brezhnev's

immediate aides could rule the country 'on Brezhnev's behalf' as long as he was still alive, they needed more time to
increase their own influence. Kosygin's illness and death
allowed them to promote Tikhonov who became Prime
Minister – a poor choice for the country but a good one for
the 'Dnepropetrovsk mafia'. Since Suslov too was ill and
unable to work a full day, Chernenko often chaired meetings of the Secretariat and the Politburo. Brezhnev's
personal apparatus, the 'Secretariat of the General Secretary',
was enlarged and became a parallel power system with
Chernenko as the Chief-of-Staff. Brezhnev was now completely dependent upon it. Some of his assistants and aides
began to act in an arrogant fashion: ministers, Republican
First Secretaries, obkom secretaries and sometimes even
members and candidate members of the Politburo were not
allowed to communicate with Brezhnev directly but had to
approach one or other of his aides first. Often the only reply
they received was from one of his assistants. This abnormal
state of affairs was one in which intrigues thrived and its
ending would have benefited everyone – except Chernenko
and his circle. However, it was difficult to predict how long
the situation might continue. Forcing Brezhnev to retire
was, of course, a possible option, but an excuse had to be
found. This was the background to the corruption scandals
which broke at the end of 1981 – especially those which
involved the Brezhnev family, the Ministry of the Interior,
and Brezhnev's ally in the KGB, General Semyon Tsvigun.

   The widespread corruption of high officials in the Soviet
Union had become a kind of 'professional illness'.[3] The
special network of privileges and services and the closely
guarded personal privacy of the high and mighty and even
the not so mighty gave their lives a somewhat artificial
quality. The distinction between personal and state property was not respected. The collapse of Gierek's regime in
Poland and the exposure of the unbelievable level of government corruption there did not pass unnoticed in the
Kremlin. In September 1980 the Central Committee of the

Soviet Communist Party passed a resolution against official corruption. Corrupt officials should be removed and exposed 'regardless of their position' (*nevziraya na litsa*). This resolution was not published in the daily press but was only distributed through the network of 'Party activists' and read at closed Party conferences and meetings. The general public was thus not invited to take part in the 'anti-corruption' drive. However, the number of articles in the press about individual cases of corruption, bribery and similar crimes committed by minor officials was increasing.

At the beginning of March 1982, foreign correspondents in Moscow began sending dispatches to their newspapers about unusual developments in Moscow criminal life involving Brezhnev's daughter Galina Churbanova, whose third husband, General Yuri Churbanov, was a Deputy Minister of Internal Affairs. The bizarre affair included the smuggling of diamonds abroad, bribery and currency speculation. Anatolii Kolevatov, the general director of the Soviet national circus, and his wife, close friends of Galina, were also implicated: some reports suggested that about 200,000 dollars and $1,000,000 worth of diamonds and other jewels were confiscated in their apartment. An intimate friend of Galina, one Boris Buryata (known as 'Boris the Gypsy' because he started out in the Moscow gypsy theatre before Galina's influence secured him a place in the Bolshoi), a minor singer at the Bolshoi Theatre, was arrested and is said to have been involved in the illegal diamond trade. Details about the scandal were apparently leaked from an official source. Other stories from Moscow indicated that the recent death of General Semyon Tsvigun was somehow linked with the Galina case and had been suicide. The name of Brezhnev's son Yuri, who was elected to the Central Committee of the Party in 1981 and was a Deputy Minister of Foreign Trade, was also mentioned. It was known, too, that the investigation of these well-connected criminals had been carried out by the KGB. The story gave some new insights into earlier indications of attempts to discredit Brezhnev.

For example, on 4 March 1982 the *Daily Telegraph* published a front-page article, 'Soviet attack on Brezhnev'. The *Observer* (7 March 1982) was more specific, with the headline 'KGB leads attack on Brezhnev mafia'. Other foreign journals, however, discussed the situation in a different light, which also seemed logical at the time. Quite a few newspapers (especially German ones), reported that the conservatives and hard-liners in the army and the KGB had started an offensive against the liberal Brezhnev group.

Later information from Moscow made it clear that Andropov was, indeed, behind the investigation of the scandal and that it was a genuine criminal case. Galina Brezhneva-Churbanova was taken to the Kremlin hospital for a time with a 'nervous breakdown'. Nobody, of course, wanted her to stand trial or even to be a witness. However no-one could have guessed that the affair would eliminate both Suslov and Tsvigun from political life.

Galina, a graduate from a Pedagogical Institute, worked for some time in the Academy of Pedagogical Sciences of the USSR. Later, she worked in the Ministry of Foreign Affairs in the section which is responsible for arranging receptions for foreigners, trips made by diplomats within the Soviet Union and entertainment for foreigners living in Moscow. It was an environment in which she had every opportunity for various kinds of unofficial deals. Her friends, naturally, exploited her position and considered her foreign connections to be absolutely safe. Nobody thought that Brezhnev's daughter, the wife of a deputy Minister of Internal Affairs, could possibly fall foul of the authorities. Corruption in these circles was quite open. However, KGB surveillance of this almost 'capitalist' island was intense, and it is certain that they could have opened the case against Galina much sooner, if it had suited their ends.

In the September 1981 issue of *Kommunist* (No. 14), the main Party journal, General Tsvigun, First Deputy Chairman of the KGB responsible for internal security and a member of Brezhnev's Dnepropetrovsk circle, published an article about the success of the KGB against the 'dissidents', whom he called criminals. Yet his own activity hardly allowed him the moral authority to pass judgement on them, for he had known about Brezhnev's daughter's affairs and connections for a long time. He had not been keen to open the case – it was too explosive – but had tried to reason with Galina, a difficult character since her student days. Eventually he had had no choice but to cover up and protect her and her friends from possible investigation. He himself did not have a reputation for honesty: he enjoyed the same expensive life-style as the other members of 'Brezhnev's mafia', and in order to gain prestige he used 'ghost writers' to publish novels on the partisan movement as well as film scenarios under his own name. One of these 'ghost writers' was Alexei Kondratovich, the former deputy editor of *Novy Mir*, dismissed in 1969 and also suspected of having been the KGB informer in the journal's office. Since his dismissal he had been badly in need of income, but his share of the royalties was not high – Tsvigun was fond of money himself.

As Brezhnev's relative Tsvigun often ignored Andropov and tried to be independent. His wife was notorious for her demand to have 'first selection' of the books at international book fairs in Moscow. These books are usually bought by the state at a great discount, but Tsvigun's wife had no intention of paying for them at all, and pretended that her husband needed them for professional reasons.

At the beginning of 1982 Andropov put the documents of the 'Circus-Kolevatov-Gypsy-Galina' case on Suslov's desk, since his permission was required for the arrest of middle-ranking Party officials. Suslov, personally, was an honest man, although during the last few years he had preferred to close his eyes to the many complaints about corruption at high levels. The Kolevatov case was too much for him to stomach – the Soviet Criminal Code actually prescribes the death penalty for economic crimes of such magnitude. Knowing what the case would mean for the Brezhnev family, he invited Tsvigun to offer an explanation, and they had an extremely heated and unpleasant discussion. According to some rumours, Suslov told Tsvigun that he would be expelled from the Party and put on trial. The next day, Tsvigun was dead, presumably having committed suicide. His obituary was not signed by any members of the Politburo, except for Andropov and other KGB officials. The confrontation also proved fatal to Suslov, an ailing man with a weak heart. After his encounter with Tsvigun he fell ill, with raised blood pressure, and the same evening he suffered a stroke. He died a few days later.

Anatolii Kolevatov, his wife, Boris the Gypsy and several other members of the coterie were arrested on the morning of Suslov's funeral while all the high officials were at Red Square. Nobody could interfere to stop the arrest and Galina was unable to contact her relatives. Later it was rumoured that both Kolevatov and Boris the Gypsy had died, one from suicide and the other from a heart attack. This may have been the case, but perhaps it was considered necessary to silence them.

This was only the beginning, for during the summer the anti-corruption drive began to touch some members of Brezhnev's Party circle. The Secretary of the Krasnodar obkom, S. F. Medunov, who used to take care of Brezhnev's dacha near Sochi, was the most prominent person affected. When his dismissal was reported in the press in August 1982,[4] many knowledgeable people in Moscow realized that this was a very close call for Brezhnev himself. Medunov's arrest (it is still a kind of 'house arrest', not detention) followed shortly after: its exact date is not clear and may have been just before Brezhnev's death or immediately following. It is important to understand why this particular arrest was of such significance. The famous Black Sea area between Sochi and Adler is full of special private dachas and villas used by high officials; Brezhnev had a large holiday complex here, at Pitsunda, built by Khrushchev. The whole area is in the Krasnodar region, and officials of the region are responsible for the provision of staff, services and other facilities. It was customary for the First and other secretaries of the obkom to be invited to the lavish parties given by the dignitaries from Moscow, and close relations were often established between them. Through their recruitment of personal staff and general supervision of the care of the guests, it was inevitable that the local Krasnodar Party and state officials should acquire a great deal of information about the private tastes and idiosyncrasies of the occupants of the 'state dachas'. Such information could prove valuable to the KGB.

Andropov's own dacha is in the Kislovodsk mineral water area of the Stavropol region in the North Caucasus, a place famous for the treatment of liver, kidney and stomach complaints. Kosygin, too, used to spend his holidays there.

On 9 November 1982 the director of the most famous food store in Moscow, Gastronom No. 2 (better known as the Jelesevskii magazin), was arrested, together with his wife who was the head of a special section of the State department store (GUM). Both were close friends of Galina Brezhneva-Churbanova.

In December the Soviet Union was due to celebrate its sixtieth anniversary. It was probably inevitable that Brezhnev would resign for reasons of health after the New Year. His attempt to gain support from the military at the unusual conference of the top army leadership in October was unsuccessful and his death came just in time to prevent more compromising disclosures.

During the funeral ceremony in the Trade Union Palace and on Red Square, Brezhnev's daughter was under the discreet escort of two KGB officers, well-dressed men who appeared to be members of the family. In the captions to the pictures of the Brezhnev family which appeared in the foreign press, they were referred to as 'unidentified men' or 'bodyguards'. The funeral was televised live, and the KGB was afraid that Galina might do, or scream, something out of place.

A few weeks later Brezhnev's son-in-law General Yuri

Churbanov was dismissed from his position as Deputy Minister of Internal Affairs and appointed head of the Murmansk department of the Ministry. This Arctic appointment must, of course, have been a disappointment to a person who had been promised a ministerial post after Shchelovkov's retirement. At the time of writing it is not yet clear whether Galina will follow her husband to Murmansk. General Churbanov is ten years younger than she is and has no children from this purely careerist marriage. With the 'Great Father-in-law' now dead, Galina possibly no longer seems a suitable wife for him.

10

Marshal Ustinov and the Military support Andropov

It proved crucial that Marshal Dmitri Ustinov not only supported Andropov in May and in November but also objected to Chernenko. Ustinov was acting both as a Politburo member and as the voice of the top military leadership; at Brezhnev's funeral he made it clear that he now held the second most important position in the Party and the country. The KGB too is a military organization (the term usually used in the West, 'secret police', is misleading). Does this mean that the Soviet leadership has been transformed into a body similar to General Wojciech Jaruzelski's military cabinet in Poland? While the answer to this question is negative, there are certainly some apparent similarities. The situation in the Soviet Union is, of course, very different from that in Poland, and there is no need for military rule. However there is a great need for an increase in discipline at all levels and for the eradication of official corruption. The efficiency of work in industry and agriculture must also be improved. The Soviet generals were in favour of a strong man at the top and Chernenko was not thought to be strong. In fact, he was unknown in military circles and this put him at a great disadvantage.

Professional military men do not play a direct role in politics in the Soviet Union. Nonetheless, the politician who receives the support of the generals and marshals is in a much stronger position in the power struggle. At several critical points in power struggles of the past (for example, the elimination of Beria in 1953 and the defeat of the plot against Khrushchev in 1957) it was the top leadership of the army which actually determined the final outcome. When Suslov and Shelepin plotted to overthrow Khrushchev in 1964, Marshal Malinovsky's support was very important. By 1964 the army was unhappy about many of Khrushchev's actions, and although Malinovsky was not a member of the Presidium, he was invited to the crucial meeting which dismissed Khrushchev, in order to demonstrate to him that the army was not on his side. After the dismissal, the army favoured Brezhnev over Suslov, who was considered to be a dogmatic politician.

Brezhnev had many good friends in the army dating from his years of service during the war; moreover, he had been the Head of the Political Directorate of the Army and Navy after Stalin's death, from March 1953 to February 1954. This does not imply that the generals considered him an authority on military affairs, but they believed – rightly, in the event – that he would be attentive to their needs and committed to strengthening the armed forces. Brezhnev did his best for the army, and his relations with the military were very good until the last years of his rule. There were no conflicts of the kind Khrushchev had from 1960 to 1964 when he tried to reduce the military budget. By 1979, however, the army had become very critical of Brezhnev's leadership. A strong army cannot coexist with a weak economy and poor agricultural performance. In addition, a significant qualitative gap had developed between the new generations of weapons systems deployed by the Soviet Union and the West: the USSR had nothing to compare with Cruise and Pershing missiles or with Trident, and American and French military planes outclassed Soviet MIGs. Notwithstanding President Reagan's statements about Soviet strategic superiority, the approximate parity which had been reached at the end of the 1970s had begun to shift in favour of the United States. Technological problems could not be solved by the army alone – they called on the general state of the country's industrial and research capabilities.

Soviet troops are stationed along the borders of the

country and also in garrisons within military districts (okrugi) which may include several regions or even republics. The army is well aware of local industrial and economic performances in these districts and is often used to tackle various problems. Thousands of military personnel take an active part in agricultural tasks, especially during the harvest, and the army is often mobilized to help with civilian construction projects such as the building of motorways and railways. In the event of a problem the local Party committee can appeal to the local army commander to send troops to do a job which should have been done by civilians – a state of affairs that is obviously viewed as unsatisfactory in military circles. Moreover, the top military leadership had become increasingly irritated by the visible corruption of Party and state officials. Although cases of corruption are not unheard of in the army, the military have less opportunity for it than their civilian counterparts, and the military elite in general has had a better record of personal honesty than that of the Party.

In addition, Brezhnev's attempts to rewrite the history of the war were a source of derision amongst the military. As his 'personality cult' became more insistent, so he was more and more often described as an outstanding military leader who had played an active part in the most important battles of the war. This was simply not true. The battle which took place near Novorossiisk in 1943, where he was the deputy of the commander for political work (the rank of commissar had been abolished in 1942) was part of a not very successful military operation and not one of the crucial battles of the war as it is depicted in works written to elevate Brezhnev's role. I am in a position to form an independent opinion about this isolated section of the Southern front (the Taman Peninsula front), for as a seventeen-year-old private in the infantry I was in the same army at the same place. By the time of the final assault which liberated Novorossiisk, in September, I was wounded and in hospital; there had been three previous unsuccessful attempts , with heavy losses.

In fact, political workers played a modest role, mostly keeping up the spirits of the soldiers. They certainly did not plan military operations or command the actual fighting. Brezhnev was promoted only once during the war. He was awarded four orders and three medals; awards of moderate distinction and quite sufficient for his military achievements. However, once he began to rise in the Party ranks after the war, he developed a desire for military prestige, and from 1965 onwards military historians attempted to trace his every move in search of actions which would merit the bestowal of new decorations. Thus, for example, a leaflet which he once wrote as a routine part of his job for the soldiers of the Eighteenth Army (or rather, which was written 'on Brezhnev's initiative') was subsequently suddenly found to have 'had a powerful mobilizing effect. It was read at meetings in all the units.'[1] Twenty-five years after the Novorossiisk battle, he was awarded the highest Soviet military medal – the Golden Star with an Order of Lenin – and the title of Hero of the Soviet Union for bravery. By 1973 he had been awarded a second gold medal for being a hero of the war and a few years later he added the gold medal of a Hero of Socialist Labour. These decorations were all awarded by decree of the Presidium of the Supreme Soviet. Once Brezhnev himself became Chairman of this Presidium, the rate at which he was awarded medals for past heroic action increased. In addition he bestowed on himself the rank of marshal, a jump over three intervening military ranks. By the time he received his third and fourth gold medals as Hero of the Soviet Union for bravery during the war it was too much – everyone knew that he was conferring the awards on himself. In fact there is even scepticism about his first 'Hero' medal. The former Soviet General Petro Grigorenko who now lives in the USA (he was deprived of citizenship while there for medical treatment) served in the same army as Brezhnev as a commander of engineering units. In his recently published *Memoirs*, he discusses Brezhnev's military records and later awards:

Everyone knows that Brezhnev did not see battle, but still they depict things as if Brezhnev had himself led an attack. He, too, remembers the past rather poorly. If he had a better memory, he would be ashamed to have received the order of Hero of the Soviet Union for participation in the battle actions of an army in which not one of the commanders or members of the military council received such an honour. They were the ones who directed the troops – not Brezhnev, whose duties were to sign party membership cards and to turn them over to new Communists. Signing battle orders was the duty of the army commander and the members of the military council . . .

Brezhnev was a rank-and-file chief of a political branch of an army. There were hundeds like him in the Soviet army forces; none participated in the direction of troops; none understood anything about such business; none would have been able to command even the lowest of all military units, a section, let alone an army. Now, if some twenty years after the end of the war one such man commences to be depicted as a great strategist and is ascribed almost the decisive role in the victory over Hitler's Germany – even though the army he served in during the whole war only served in minor ways – then the role and glory ascribed to him is such drivel that it is shameful even to have to refute it. But when such drivel is disseminated and the hero himself accepts it with gladness and begins to believe in his own outstanding role, it says something . . . about the intellectual capabilities of the 'hero'.[2]

The top military commanders were certainly irritated by this exaggeration of Brezhnev's wartime role. They knew what was usually required for the award of these decorations, and were most deeply offended when Brezhnev awarded himself the Order of Victory. This was a special decoration bestowed on only one occasion to honour a few famous Soviet marshals like Zhukov and Rokossovsky immediately after the war. It was intended only for field commanders of whole fronts or of groups of fronts who had successfully planned and executed large-scale battles. Marshal

Zhukov, for example, was awarded the Victory Medal for the final assault on Berlin by the front which he commanded. The medal is a large and beautiful decoration of gold and platinum and it is not difficult to understand why Brezhnev should have coveted it for his collection. But by presenting it to himself he devalued military decorations in general. An unknown military figure at the end of the war, he now had more medals than Marshal Georgi Zhukov himself, the man who began his war service by fighting against the Japanese in 1939 and concluded it by capturing Berlin, who had organized the defence of Leningrad in September 1941, the defence of Moscow from October to December 1941 and the first offensive in December 1941 which drove the German army from the city, and had been one of the commanders in the Stalingrad battle. Comparisons with Khrushchev also suggested themselves. Khrushchev had spent most of the war in the political structure of the army and as a member of the military councils. He had attained the rank of general, and had taken an active part in the planning of some of the major battles, notably the crucial battle for Stalingrad and the liberation of Kiev. Yet when he died in 1971 he had received only 27 medals and awards – about 10 per cent of Brezhnev's tally. These absurdities contributed to the growing disillusionment of the military with Brezhnev's leadership.

The army was not displeased by the war in Afghanistan. For the top military leadership it represented a good testing and training ground, and for many officers service in Afghanistan was a way of obtaining valuable experience and faster promotion. However, the disastrous performance of Soviet equipment in Lebanon in the summer of 1982 (particularly aircraft and anti-aircraft missiles) affected the relationship between the top military men and the government very badly. The military blamed the slow modernization of the Soviet arms and defence industries for this poor showing. Unusually, a meeting was held in October of the top military and top Party leadership to try to improve relations between the two groups. Although Brezhnev promised improvements, neither his speech nor his senile appearance made a good impression. It was clear that he would not live long enough to honour his promises.

Chernenko, Brezhnev's protégé, had no authority amongst the military leaders. He had spent the war years as Party secretary in the Krasnoyarsk region of Siberia, far from the front, and it was thought that he did not understand military problems. On the other hand Andropov, as head of the KGB, had worked very closely with the army. The KGB is responsible for guarding all important military objects and missile launching sites, and fifteen specially trained divisions of frontier guards form the largest part of its personnel. The army cannot fire nuclear missiles without the KGB, as their officers form part of the launching teams. During the fifteen years that Andropov was in charge, he took part in the preparation of many joint military–KGB operations and worked closely with top army generals and marshals. Soviet military actions abroad like the invasion of Czechoslovakia in 1968, operations in Angola in 1975, in Ethiopia, and in Afghanistan inevitably required the close co-operation of the military and the political intelligence provided by the KGB. If the reports of KGB defectors like Vladimir Kuzichkin are to be believed, it was Brezhnev who argued in favour of intervention in Afghanistan, while the KGB had serious doubts about the operation.[3] When these doubts proved to be justified, the army in Afghanistan did not blame the KGB for their difficulties but rather Brezhnev's faction which had ignored the KGB assessment.

In Stalin's time there was deep mistrust between the army and the security services. The best officers, generals and marshals were arrested by the security services in 1936–38, and about 90 per cent of the most seasoned and experienced divisional and army commanders were executed or died in the Gulag before the war. This was a terrible blow to the morale and fighting capacity of the Soviet army and it contributed to the defeats and losses of 1941 and 1942.

During the war the notorious 'special departments' and security detachments (*zagrad otryady*) kept army commanders under permanent surveillance and threat, effectively reducing their initiative and manoeuvrability. This produced a permanent hostility between the army and the NKVD services similar to the hostility between the German regular army, the SS troops, and the Gestapo. Neither Hitler nor Stalin trusted their regular troops, and both created a special military police which was above the law.

Although the situation changed radically under Khrushchev, who gave the army much greater freedom of action, even he feared their independence and a possible military takeover. This was why, without any valid reason, he suddenly dismissed Marshal Zhukov from his position as Defence Minister while Zhukov was on an official visit abroad. The new minister, Marshal Malinovsky, was neither a prominent figure nor very popular in the army. While Andropov was head of the KGB, however, the relationship between the army and the KGB changed from one of hostility to one of partnership. In addition to performing its security role, the KGB began to provide the army with intelligence, logistic support, assessments, highly trained frontier troops and special assault units trained in the languages of the countries bordering the Soviet Union and often belonging to the same ethnic groups.

The professional military are well represented in the Central Committee, which numbers thirty marshals and generals among its members and candidate members. They form a smaller lobby than the regional Party secretaries or the technocrats, but they are far more united. Within the Politburo Marshal Andrei Grechko was a very strong supporter of Brezhnev's policy (including the 'Brezhnev Doctrine'), and an old personal friend. When he died in 1976 there was no obvious professional military candidate for the post of Minister of Defence. The replacement of the old generation by the new in the army had taken place in the 1970s – military commanders could not, like political leaders, be kept at their posts until their natural death. Although the present military leadership has in fact had real combat experience, most of its members were in their twenties or thirties during the war and served as captains, majors or colonels. Marshal Ustinov, appointed Minister of Defence after Grechko's death, is not a professional military man but a talented engineer and artillery designer, a minister of the armament industry during the war and an able and competent administrator. He was made a First Deputy Prime Minister in 1957. There were rumours that he might be elected Brezhnev's successor, and he seemed to be a strong candidate for Kosygin's post when the latter became too ill to continue as Prime Minister. But by 1982 Ustinov's age was against him and the role of 'kingmaker' was more to his liking. His support for Andropov proved crucial. Personally, he is known to be honest, hard-working and a disciplinarian: with such qualities he would hardly have been pleased if Brezhnev's 'Dnepropetrovsk mafia' had inherited power. His resolute objection to Chernenko's promotion affected the way others voted. The election of a leader who did not have the backing of the army would have been a poor choice, particularly at the time of a new Cold War.

Western 'Kremlinologists' failed to understand the change which took place in the relationship of the army to the KGB during the decade before Brezhnev's death. Discussing the succession problem in April 1982, the *Newsweek* team of 'Sovietologists' dismissed Andropov's chances because of possible opposition from the army:

> But a bid for succession by Andropov would possibly face strong opposition from the Soviet military. The KGB and the armed forces are often rivals, and Russia's military leaders have generally held a veto during Kremlin shake-ups. If they choose to wield the veto this time, Brezhnev's Defense Minister, Dmitry Ustinov, 73, could emerge as a dark-horse contender.[4]

When Vitalii Fedorchuk was appointed head of the KGB

in May 1982, he immediately made it clear that the KGB is part of the military force rather than a 'secret police'. His first directive enforced the compulsory wearing of KGB military uniform for all staff members, some of whom had never worn uniform before. He proceeded to cancel the second day off for KGB personnel, following the practice which applies in the army. The army and the KGB were ready for the inevitable succession of Party leadership.

11

The New Man at the Top

Even if some Moscow intellectuals and a few astute Western journalists and experts on Soviet affairs were expecting Andropov to inherit Brezhnev's mantle, most of the rest of the world was taken by surprise. The American administration, according to the *Wall Street Journal*, had long assumed that the Soviet leader was near death. When his death was reported, 'few of the middle and upper-level officials concerned with US–Soviet affairs bothered to rush to their offices on Veterans' Day, a federal holiday'.[1] There was clearly no expectation of rapid change, and very little information about Brezhnev's likely successor. The *Wall Street Journal* went on to state that

> Reagan administration officials candidly conceded they know little for sure about who would succeed Mr Brezhnev. They assume the succession struggle will take months, or even a year, and that Soviet policy won't change much soon.[2]

To the general public in the Soviet Union and even to the majority of ordinary Party members, who know very little about members of the Politburo, Andropov's election was unexpected. His KGB background was not an encouraging omen. When Stalin died in 1953, Khrushchev was already a popular figure – his speeches in the Ukraine in the late 1940s and in Moscow in 1950–52 had been imaginative and fresh, concerned with people's needs. During the last years of Stalin's rule, when Khrushchev was First Secretary of the

Moscow Party Committee, he used to visit factories and local meetings, where he would make spontaneous speeches and mix with people, and be received with genuine enthusiasm. He enjoyed the confidence of the general public much more than Stalin's other, more bureaucratic associates did. Brezhnev did not have this kind of popularity in 1964, but he was at least a familiar figure. He had held the post of Chairman of the Presidium of the Supreme Soviet for four years, a post previously filled by esteemed figures such as Mikhail Kalinin and Kliment Voroshilov, and one which traditionally involved a certain amount of public exposure. The Presidium of the Supreme Soviet confirms all laws and important awards and almost all complaints are addressed to its Chairman: therefore when Brezhnev became Party leader he was not an unknown quantity and his election was accepted as natural.

The situation was very different when Brezhnev died. His death was preceded by the death of the two other publicly recognized Politburo members, Kosygin and Suslov. Podgorny had been dismissed in 1977. Neither Andropov nor Chernenko occupied positions which gave them access to the general public: the appearances they made were on traditional occasions, when one or the other would make a general speech modelled on the familiar pattern. When it was announced that the General Secretary of the CPSU was Yuri Vladimirovich Andropov, people were avid for information about him. Within two days, Andropov's *Selected Speeches and Articles*[3] printed in an edition of 100,000 in 1979 and collecting dust on the shelves of Soviet bookshops, had been sold out.

To set this publication in its context it must be explained that one of the privileges granted to members and candidate members of the Politburo to enable them to gain public notice is the entitlement to publish a collection of their speeches and articles (usually carefully selected to omit those past speeches they themselves would prefer to forget). When Brezhnev began to publish his memoirs, other Politburo members also brought out their collections, which all appeared in 1979–80, published by Politizdat. Brezhnev's works (which mainly consisted of speeches) appeared in seven volumes; Kosygin's and Suslov's in two. Many of the speeches, of course, were shortened and altered: in those made before 1953 all praise of Stalin was removed, while all mention of Khrushchev disappeared from those from the period 1953–64. Where it was impossible to remove Khrushchev's name (for example, from speeches made at the Party Plenums discussing his reforms, or at the Twenty-Second Party Congress), the speeches were simply omitted. Other Politburo members published enormously thick one-volume collections (Kirilenko's, for instance, numbered 759 pages, while Grishin's, Romanov's, Shcherbitsky's and Ponomarev's all ran to more than 600), so Andropov's mere 318 pages made his book – along with Pel'she's – the slimmest. The edition of 100,000 in which it was printed was not, in fact, very large by Soviet standards. A significant number of copies would be distributed to libraries and Party organizations. Until Andropov's election as leader the sales of his book had actually been very low. The pages of his official speeches were, indeed, a poor source of information about the man himself. Some of them date from Andropov's work in the Karelo-Finnish Republic; collectively they only prove that his public pronouncements and articles were not very different from those of other leaders.

If the news of Brezhnev's death was received without emotion by the Soviet public, Andropov's election met with no enthusiasm. The first gloomy anecdote to circulate was probably an accurate reflection of the general feeling: Andropov explains to a foreign journalist that he is sure the people will follow him. 'And those who don't follow me, will follow Brezhnev.' A later anecdote maintains that the Kremlin will probably be renamed the Andropolis.

When Chernenko proposed Andropov as General Secretary, he urged the Politburo to maintain the Brezhnev line, and as long as Brezhnev was lying in state, the Brezhnev line was followed. But as soon as the mountain of flowers covering the fresh grave began to fade, the pillars of 'Brezhnevism' began to fall. They have not all crumbled at once: the Soviet system of government requires leadership through consensus and this means that radical change is unlikely. But at sixty-eight Andropov is the oldest man to take on the task of running the Soviet Union and he cannot afford to be too slow. Moreover, his position is far stronger than those of his predecessors, who had to face power struggles after they had been chosen as leader. By November 1982 Andropov had no challengers or rivals, and he had a clear mandate for change. He had the support of the men who did most to make him General Secretary: Marshal Ustinov and Vladimir Scherbitsky, with Gromyko, Gorbachev, Kunaev and Aliyev forming a subsidiary group. The leading men may change with time – there will be new Central Committee Plenums in 1983, and then and at the next Party Congress, which will probably be convened earlier than 1986 when it is due, the Party leadership will almost certainly be rejuvenated. But Andropov's position in the Politburo is strong enough already to show the Soviet people and the world that it is not only the style but also the substance of Soviet internal and foreign policy that is changing.

Part Three

Andropov in Power

12

Forming a Team

The death of Kosygin in 1980 and of Suslov and Brezhnev in 1982 marked not only the passing away of three of the most important figures of the post-Khrushchev era but the passing of a political generation. The retirement of Kirilenko confirmed this. Although the new General Secretary is not a young man and neither are his closest supporters, the seventy-three-year-old Ustinov and sixty-four-year-old Shcherbitsky, they are unlikely to follow Brezhnev's policy of life tenure for those who occupy the highest and most demanding positions. But the replacement of the top ruling group cannot take place very quickly in the Soviet Union, for the system works on the basis of a general consensus among the leading members of the Central Committee and the government, not through free elections at regular intervals which can change the composition of the party in power or replace it altogether.

At the Plenum of the Central Committee which has held just before the budget session of the Supreme Soviet at the end of November, only Kirilenko's retirement was announced, and even this had been expected well before Brezhnev's death. Even the eighty-three-year-old Arvid Pelshe, who had been rumoured dead for two weeks in November, and the eighty-one-year-old candidate member of the Politburo Vasilii Kuznetsov did not retire. This was not because they were still doing their work well but because the few days between Brezhnev's funeral and the already scheduled Plenum were not long enough to find appropriate replacements. The Plenum promoted the fifty-nine-year-old Aliyev to full membership of the Politburo and appointed N. I. Ryshkov as a new Secretary of the Central Committee. It is important to note that Ryshkov was not appointed to either of the positions vacated by Andropov and Kirilenko, which were left vacant. A young man of fifty-three and an able technocrat, formerly the successful director of the largest industrial complex in the USSR, Uralmash, he was charged with creating a new department of the Central Committee to co-ordinate the work of the other industrial departments and to develop new, more effective methods of management in different branches of industry. Ryshkov's department is to set up a new system of interaction between all branches of industry and Gosplan, the Prices and Salary Committee, etc. It is intended to co-ordinate the industrial life of the country as far as is possible. In theory Ryshkov's aim will be to reduce waste and overproduction in some branches of industry and increase production in others. Under the Soviet economic system, the transfer of funds and materials from one branch of industry to another is traditionally a long, painful, inefficient, bureaucratic affair. It is hoped that this new co-ordinating development will be able to devise some short-cuts.

The creation of this department and the appointment of Ryshkov as its head confirmed my expectation that Andropov would concentrate on economic performance rather than on liberal reforms. I did not think that the kind of 'thaw' which heralded Khrushchev's rule was likely. Although Brezhnev was a conservative leader, he was not a tyrant in the Stalin tradition and in a political sense his regime was comparatively mild. The general public complained mostly about muddle and economic anarchy, not about the repressions, which were aimed at dissidents and not at ordinary workers and farmers.

The session of the Supreme Soviet which opened on 23 November 1982 brought even fewer surprises. Of course, it was impossible to change the budget at such short notice.

The main excitement was about the vacant position of the nominal 'President', i.e. the Chairman of the Presidium of the Supreme Soviet, which had earlier been promised to Chernenko as a consolation prize in the power struggle. This position does not carry any real influence, since the Chairman cannot make personal decisions: he (or she) merely presides over the forty-member Presidium which, according to the Constitution, is the 'collective President'. But it does have some ceremonial importance, and is convenient for the pursuance of an active foreign policy if it is combined with the job of General Secretary – a discovery made by Brezhnev. This is why the Moscow diplomatic community as well as Kremlin watchers abroad expected Andropov to take this position so as to increase his own prestige and power. To everyone's great surprise, it remained vacant. Andropov was elected to the Presidium as an ordinary member, but this was simply protocol for the leader of the Party. The failure to elect a new President was no disadvantage from his point of view, but was actually an indication of his rapidly consolidated power, which allowed him to ignore the promise made to Chernenko. It was a defeat for the 'Brezhnevites'. Being Chairman of the Supreme Soviet could, in fact, have proved a waste of time for Andropov if he meant to do business rather than preside over ceremonies. It was wise, therefore, to keep this position open for the time being. Later it can be offered to someone completely loyal and popular with the general public, someone like Gromyko if he decides to retire from his stressful diplomatic job, or Tikhonov as compensation for his retirement from the Premiership.

The one new executive appointment which attracted attention was Aliyev's appointment as First Deputy Prime Minister. Although the Prime Minister has several 'First' and several ordinary deputies, as a Politburo member Aliyev became the most influential figure in the government. This was a wise appointment – Aliyev is a tough man, a good administrator, personally honest and a representative of the

substantial Soviet Moslem population. It is not important
that he himself is not a religious man: in the eyes of the
Moslem world he is a Moslem, not Geidar Aliyev, but
Geider-Ali Ali-Zadeh. As a colonel, he served as deputy to
General Tsvigun, the head of the KGB in Azerbaijan. When
Tsvigun moved to Moscow in 1967 to become First Deputy
Chairman of the KGB, Aliyev was recommended to succeed
him. This was indicative of the trust Tsvigun placed in him,
for it was unusual for a native to be appointed boss of the
KGB in one of the Union Republics. In 1969, when the level
of corruption in Azerbaijan became intolerable, Brezhnev
reluctantly dismissed the First Secretary of the Azerbaijan
Central Committee, Veli Akhundov. Akhundov, a physician
by profession, became Vice-President of the Azerbaijan
Academy of Sciences and Aliyev was appointed in his place.
So successful did he prove that it was jokingly said that he
had 'restored Soviet power' in Azerbaijan. The rate of
economic development there, previously below average for
the Soviet Union, increased remarkably: in 1975–80 the
increase in GNP in the USSR as a whole was 24 per cent
while in Azerbaijan it was 47 per cent. Aliyev had thus
proved himself to be an intelligent man capable of making
adventurous, pioneering decisions.

Aliyev's promotion was immediately perceived by foreign
observers as a new initiative to regain 'Moscow's lost
influence in the Moslem world'.[1] This may be true, but it
was certainly not the main reason for his appointment.
Andropov seems to have decided to reduce all forms of
nationalism, particularly 'Great Russian nationalism',
which would ease relations with many countries and not
just with the Moslem world. China, for instance, has used
the revival of Russian nationalism as a standard explanation
for Soviet actions abroad. Aliyev is popular in Middle-
Eastern Marxist circles. Although loyal to Brezhnev –
Brezhnev and Tsvigun were originally responsible for his
promotion – his was a loyalty of expediency. His eloquent
praise of Brezhnev on public occasions was an Eastern kind

of subtle flattery rather than sincere admiration. As a professional KGB officer before 1969, he is likely to find it easier to work with Andropov than he would have found working with Chernenko.

Aliyev's first priority is to improve the Soviet transport system – the bottleneck of the economy. In a country as large as the Soviet Union, good rail and motorway systems are extremely important but have been neglected for many years. In his first speech at the Central Committee Plenum, a reasonably short, businesslike speech, Andropov had singled out the transport system for special criticism. A few days later the Minister of Railways, Ivan Pavlovsky, was dismissed and his First Deputy, the fifty-five-year-old Nikolai Konarev, was promoted to replace him. In previous years ministerial changes had usually been reported on the last page of the newspapers in a short 'Khronika' (Chronicle) section. Konarev's appointment was reported on the front pages of the central press together with a photograph and a brief biography, apparently to increase his authority and to show the general public that he was the right man for the job. This new publicity was an interesting innovation, and it was repeated for subsequent important appointments at ministerial level and the level of Chairman of a State Committee. The forty-nine-year-old Boris Pastukhov was the next person to be promoted, to the Chairmanship of the Committee for Publishing, a position he inherited from Boris Stukalin, one of Suslov's men and a rather conservative individual. Stukalin in turn was promoted, to a post where his ideological vigilance would find better use, as the head of the propaganda department of the Central Committee, the department which instructs the large army of Party ideologists in the regions and districts and also has general responsibility for the media. This transfer might be a signal that ideological work is to be carried out more energetically in future. A change that did not attract attention was the dismissal of Stepan Khitrov, Minister for Construction of Agricultural Enterprises.

Khitrov was an old man of seventy-two and his ministry was notorious for its poor performance.

It must be added, however, that the prospect of more 'open' government which the increased publicity for individuals and the published reports of Politburo meetings appeared to herald seemed to be belied when the annual report for 1982 failed to include the main figures for agricultural production. Restrictions on reporting statistics were introduced in 1981, when the figures for grain and other agricultural products were omitted, probably because they were embarrassingly low. Although agricultural production improved in 1982, again no figures appeared. This sensitivity is misguided, for if foreign experts or the local population have insufficient information, they are likely to draw the most pessimistic conclusions.

The next important reshuffle took place on 17 December when the seventy-two-year-old General Shchelokov was replaced as Minister of Internal Affairs. Shchelokov was not only an old Brezhnev man from the Dnepropetrovsk days but had also been very lenient with cases of official corruption, even when they were quite blatant. Personally he too was corrupt, though the general public was, of course, unaware of this. There were several steep price rises in the Soviet Union between 1970 and 1982 for luxury items like gold, silver, jewellery, caviar and furs, and Shchelokov's wife used to warn their friends well beforehand so that they could buy large quantities before the price increases 'unexpectedly' came into force. Apparently Party officials and the KGB knew about these 'leaks', which would sometimes set off a chain reaction so that certain shops would be swamped by anxious buyers. However they were powerless to act, because of Shchelokov's close relationship with Brezhnev.

The emigration and foreign travel service (OVIR), officially a section of the Ministry of Internal Affairs, was notorious for accepting bribes. Every motorist knew about corruption in the police inspectorate of cars, and the public reputation of the police (militia) was generally very low. Officially, cities like Moscow, Kiev and Leningrad are not 'open' in the sense of being allowed to increase in size freely: people who wish to live there need a special police residence registration permit, a *propiska*. Nonetheless the population of all the capital cities continued to grow, because a *propiska* could be bought if one could afford the price. It can be argued that this 'second' economy, the 'moonlighting' which is such a prevalent feature of Soviet life, benefits rather than harms the Soviet population, since it makes available certain goods and services which the state is not yet able to provide. It is certainly not corruption, in the usual meaning of the word, since it contributes to the GNP in the same way as private peasant plots and allotments contribute to the production of food. Police corruption, however, is a different matter: it creates public discontent and reduces the general working discipline of the population.

It was no surprise, then, when Shchelokov was dismissed. What was a surprise was that Vitalii Fedorchuk, the recently appointed head of the KGB, was made the new Minister of Internal Affairs. He was replaced by his deputy at the KGB, Viktor Chebrikov, who had been Andropov's First Deputy as well. Chebrikov, aged fifty-nine and a member of the Central Committee, might have been considered the natural choice for Andropov's job in May, but he was identified as a friend of Tsvigun and a supporter of Brezhnev. Although younger than the rest of the 'Brezhnev mafia', he had graduated from the same college as Brezhnev – the Dnepropetrovsk Metallurgical Institute, which a number of other high officials, including Tikhonov and Shchelokov, had also attended – and, again like Brezhnev, had begun his Party career in the Dnepropetrovsk region. He was appointed a KGB deputy chairman in 1967, during reorganization, together with G. K. Zinev, a member of the same circle. It is likely that someone close to Brezhnev had recommended him for the position. Although Chebrikov was thus identified as a trusted adherent of Brezhnev, it appears that, by

December 1982, the question of loyalty to the former General Secretary was no longer considered relevant: what was primarily important for Andropov was that Chebrikov was an able man whom he knew well and could count upon for full co-operation. Certainly Andropov did not want to create the impression that there was something fundamentally amiss in the KGB hierarchy. For Fedorchuk, the Ministry of Internal Affairs represented a promotion. The MVD is a larger organization than the KGB and more in the public eye, and the title of Minister is still considered to be superior to that of Chairman of a State Committee. More interesting, perhaps, is the fact that both branches of the security organs are now in the hands of men who will be attentive to Andropov and who, as members of the professional military establishment, are unlikely to have political ambitions. They know why they have been chosen for their particular posts and they also know that if they do not perform well they can only be demoted. There can be no promotion. Brezhnev treated Shchelokov like an old friend, almost a relative. Andropov will treat his new security chiefs as subordinates who must understand what discipline means. These changes are important signals that can hardly be misinterpreted. All three important promotions – of Aliyev, Fedorchuk and Chebrikov – have been of professional KGB men from its military branch.

Another important task for the new leader was to form an inner circle of advisers and aides, a personal staff. The 'Secretariat to the General Secretary' was a body created by Brezhnev. Khrushchev had several personal aides (for agriculture, culture, etc.), but they did not form a definite administrative structure. Some were on secondment from various government organizations, others were Party department staff members. Stalin had only one personal secretary, A. I. Poskrebyshev, but he treated everyone, including members of the Politburo, as his personal retinue. A full list of aides and assistants is never given in official documents, but one can sometimes establish who is in this circle by looking at official communiqués. Often a list given of people who have attended a particular meeting will include the name of someone designated 'assistant to the General Secretary'. From Andropov's first meetings with foreign dignitaries it was clear that A. M. Aleksandrov-Agentov had preserved (or regained) his position as adviser. A new, hitherto unknown name, V. V. Sharapov, also appeared as an adviser who was present at Andropov's meetings with socialist leaders. Sharapov had earlier worked for *Pravda* and in the press department of the Central Committee. Other Brezhnev aides have not been invited to continue their functions. A Moscow source said in December that they continued to receive their salaries and to have access to their offices, but they had no work to do. Andropov seems to require fewer aides than Brezhnev did. He has already made it clear that his speeches will be short, businesslike and relatively infrequent. Brezhnev could not deliver any speech, no matter how short, without a prepared written text – even when he had to make a short toast at a diplomatic dinner, the text was prepared and memorized in advance both by him and by his interpreter. Often Brezhnev forgot whole sentences, but his excellent official interpreter would remember the original text and translate that, rather than Brezhnev's actual words. Andropov is certainly a better conversationalist, and can express his views to foreigners without any difficulty as he demonstrated at the reception for foreign dignitaries after Brezhnev's funeral.

Everybody expected that the next person to retire would be Tikhonov, now seventy-seven. Apart from having been close to Brezhnev, he was simply too old and weak to continue as Premier. The problem now is not the sequence of retirements – there are quite a few elderly people around – but who should be appointed to such important positions. The testing of the qualities of possible candidates may take several months. Andropov needs changes which will improve the performance of the administration and help to achieve his first priority – to reduce waste, corruption and inefficiency. He has no choice but to appoint people of the younger generation. However, the most important negative effect of Brezhnev's life-tenure policy was to create a serious shortage of experienced cadres. Younger men and women in the Party and state administration have been kept at middle-level positions for too long, so that few of those who are now in their forties or fifties have the necessary experience for a really senior job.

Before Brezhnev's death, Roy Medvedev published a number of articles in which he analysed the profile of the next generation of Soviet leaders.[2] He came to the conclusion that the people who are about to take power from the old leaders

> . . . have advanced in their careers very slowly. They were kept, and are still being kept, too long at relatively minor posts. They do not have sufficient experience to solve problems on a national and international scale.[3]

He goes on to ask:

> Will they be able to acquire it quickly enough? Will they be able to boldly promote to responsible positions people even younger and more active than they are? Or, having waited themselves so long for promotion, will they be even more intolerant toward the younger generation?[4]

It is very difficult to answer this question on the basis of the government and Party replacements made in January. It was natural, for example, that after very serious criticisms in the press about the deplorable state of Soviet internal trade (characterized by inefficiency, waste and corruption) the Minister of Internal Trade, Aleksandr Struyev, who was seventy-six and had held his position since 1965, was forced to retire. But the newly appointed minister, Grigorii Vashchenko, at sixty-two also belongs to the older generation. On the other hand, in Brezhnev's time it was usual to replace retired ministers by one of their deputies. Grigorii Vashchenko, however, was brought to Moscow from the

Ukraine where he was a Deputy Prime Minister. This could mean a shake-up in the Ministry of Trade, probably one of the most corrupt ministries in the government system. The dismissal of the fifty-two-year-old Valentin Makeyev from his post as a Deputy Prime Minister on 19 January and his appointment to a less responsible position in the Soviet Trade Union Council is more difficult to explain, for Makeyev had only occupied his post in the government for two years. He was a protégé of Victor Grishin – for four years (1976–80) he was Grishin's right-hand man as the Second Secretary of the Moscow City Committee of the CPSU.

On 11 January 1983 Tikhon Kiselyev, First Secretary of the Byelorussian Communist Party and a candidate member of the Poliburo, died after a long illness. In Brezhnev's time it would have been usual for somebody from the Byelorussian Politburo or Secretariat to be chosen to succeed him. When the previous Byelorussian Party chief Pyotr Masherov died in a traffic accident in 1980, Kiselyev was the Byelorussian Prime Minister. As this was the second most important position in the Republic, it was natural for him to become Masherov's successor. However, only two days after Kiselyev's death Andropov pressed the Byelorussian Central Committee Plenum to elect as First Secretary a man sent to them from Moscow, N. N. Slunkov, an unknown figure. Slunkov was not even a member or candidate member of the Central Committee of the Party; his last position in Moscow had been as a Deputy Chairman of Gosplan, although he had previously worked in Byelorussia. In general his appointment was seen as a sign that changes had to be made in Byelorussia, which borders on Poland and is the third most populous Republic of the Soviet Union, but one of its poorer ones.

It seems that Brezhnev's custom of replacing retired or deceased officials with their deputies, a source of stability but also the best way to cover up any mismanagement or corruption, is now over. For an outsider Slunkov's appointment may appear insignificant. But it was a clear signal to all First Secretaries in all the Republics and regions and to their deputies. They must clean up their provinces before somebody new arrives from Moscow to do it for them.

13

Andropov's Economic Programme

Khrushchev and Brezhnev both started their terms in office by formulating their economic priorities. Both men inherited many serious economic problems which had accumulated during the last few years of the previous leadership. The concentration of power in the hands of one person and the creation of a personality cult apparently coincided with a deterioration in industrial and agricultural management and a general decline in living standards. In the case of Stalin's rule in 1949–53, it was mostly the peasants whose living standards fell, but during the last few years of Khrushchev's era difficulties began to appear for the urban as well as the rural population. The same pattern appeared during Brezhnev's last years, when the consolidation of his personal power and the creation of his personality cult in 1977–82 coincided with a decline in the growth rate in industry, a general decline in agriculture and the development of chronic food shortages, mostly because of an imbalance between the rapid growth of the urban population and stagnation in agriculture despite large investments. In Stalin's time the peasants were brutally exploited. Under Brezhnev they were subsidized, but the problems remained the same – the rural areas were unable to produce enough food to maintain reasonably good supplies to cities and towns. In the 1920s and 1930s there was a bread shortage; by the 1970s and 1980s the problem was no longer bread but meat and the quality of diet. The demands of the new, more educated and more sophisticated generation were not satisfied, and the level of discontent increased towards the end of Brezhnev's life. The economy, therefore, and primarily the consumer-oriented economy, had to be a priority for the new post-Brezhnev leadership as well. However, Khrushchev's task in 1953 and Brezhnev's in 1964 had been easier by comparison because the whole economic structure of society then was much simpler. By 1982 the Soviet Union was a modern 'superpower' with an extremely complex economic system. On the other hand, the economic situation in 1982 could hardly be described as in 'crisis': the Soviet Union was already a highly developed country, and its problems were essentially those of a consumer society. What was needed was a reassessment of priorities, some modifications and an improvement of management. People in the country and in towns lived reasonably well, but they could live even better and they knew this. It was this awareness which was the main source of discontent.

Soviet economic problems are quite different from those of the Western industrialized countries and, of course, different again from those of the poor developing nations of the Third World. The Western media often distort the economic situation in the Soviet Union, out of ignorance or for reasons of propaganda, yet these distortions are so common that Western politicians begin to believe them and make serious political miscalculations which later prove an embarrassment. Good examples of this are President Carter's grain embargo and President Reagan's embargo on the Siberian gas pipeline – both more damaging to the American than to the Soviet economy.

Ever since Stalin's time, the main problem of the Soviet economic system has been the disproportion between its different branches. The annual growth rate has usually been very high (by average Western standards, higher than in the United States or Britain), but uneven. Khrushchev managed to improve the serious imbalance between industry and agriculture which he inherited from Stalin, but he did not succeed in overcoming it. Brezhnev's and Kosygin's measures produced a more balanced economy. Between 1965 and 1980 the growth in industrial output was substantial, by 270 per cent, but agricultural production grew by only 35 per cent, and in 1981 declined slightly because of adverse weather conditions. In 1982 it showed only a small increase, of 3–4 per cent over the 1981 figure, well below target. Between 1965 and 1982 the population also grew by about 35 per cent, but more than half of this growth was in towns. Clearly, therefore, the per capita production of food for the urban population actually declined, making it necessary to purchase significant amounts of grain and other food products abroad. The increase in foreign imports could, fortunately, be financed by sales of oil and gas – the substantial rise in world prices for these energy resources was extremely beneficial to the Soviet Union, which is the world's largest producer of oil and gas.

Like new leaders all over the world, Andropov has the great advantage of being personally dissociated from responsibility for *past* problems. In his first policy speech at the Central Committee Plenum on 22 November 1982, he made only a limited number of critical remarks, but even these were treated as a 'fresh approach' by the foreign press. Brezhnev always began by talking about achievements; Andropov preferred to do without this routine praise of economic successes. However, the claims in the foreign press that he had 'told the Soviet people bluntly that their system was faltering and that he had no "ready recipes" for getting it moving again'[1] were far-fetched. Andropov did not blame 'the system' and it was not in his interests to do so. He divided the responsibility for the country's weak economic performance equally between the government and the workers and farmers themselves. It was necessary for him to do this since his 'recipe' is not only to improve management but also to make workers and peasants work harder and more effectively and to improve labour discipline.

Industrial growth was only 2.8 per cent in 1982. The Plan had envisaged 4 per cent growth for industry and 2.7 per cent for the GNP as a whole. The 1983 plan which was recommended by the Plenum and accepted by the Supreme Soviet was not much more ambitious – 3.2 per cent growth for industry and 3.3 per cent for the GNP. But Andropov's main problem is not production levels. He was uncompromising in his insistence that everything which is produced or harvested should be made available or preserved, for he is well aware that a lot of goods which are produced, and which are registered in the statistics, are subsequently lost or are useless because of poor quality. The priorities which he set out in his speech were to improve management, to increase productivity (which means harder work and better discipline) and to improve the quality of both labour and goods. He also called for acceleration in the rate at which new technology and methods of planning are introduced and emphasized the need to reduce losses and waste. He had no new ideas to offer for agriculture, merely stressing the importance of following the 'Food Programme' introduced in May 1982. There was nothing really 'reform-minded' about his speech – it was, after all, impossible for him to suggest anything radically new only one week after taking office. He needed to show people that developments would be in the right direction without promising too much, and this he accomplished.

In December 1982 the reorganized Ministry of Railways and other transport systems presented a new programme to improve transportation which was accepted by the Central Committee and the Council of Ministers and published in all central Soviet newspapers on 15 December 1982. The main emphasis in the programme was on improving co-ordination between all the transportation systems: the railways, merchant fleet, river transportation system, air cargo and road freight transport, which are all under different ministries and had previously been poorly co-ordinated. Significant technical improvements of all the means of transportation were envisaged, as well as higher salaries for workers and a link between the income of employees and the overall economic performance of the transport system. The fact that only three weeks elapsed between the initial criticisms, the replacement of the Minister, and the preparation of a new, complex and well co-ordinated programme of improvements suggests that the slow-moving government bureaucratic machine has started to work more rapidly than in the past.

As soon as Andropov was elected General Secretary, most serious Western journals and newspapers suggested that as an admirer of the Hungarian economic system he might introduce some elements from the Hungarian model into the Soviet Union. I am rather sceptical about the likelihood of this happening in the immediate future. Perhaps, *after* visible improvements have taken place in the basic industries, some elements of private initiative will be encouraged in the service sector. Abroad, Andropov will reject any attempts to link trade with other countries with political conditions even more energetically than Brezhnev did. The refusal of the Soviet Union to buy American grain above the modest fixed quota stipulated in the previous agreement, the effective rejection of Reagan's offer of extra supplies, and the similar refusal to buy surplus Common Market butter offered on terms inferior to those offered to other purchasers, all indicate that Andropov will follow the traditional Soviet approach, probably making it even more explicit. It is likely that the new leadership will try to make an overall reduction in the amount of food purchased abroad.

More food is probably lost every year because of the shortage of refrigeration space and storage facilities, the inadequate number of special rail carriages and refrigerated lorries, etc. than the USSR buys abroad. Efforts to reduce waste were immediate and striking. Soviet newspapers stopped describing the achievements of the best collective farms (under Brezhnev the hope was that such descriptions would encourage emulation) and turned their attention to criticism of inefficient farms and incompetence in the food industry. In just one issue of *Izvestiya*, for example, there were three front-page stories about waste and the loss of food – in the trade network, in the transport system because of the lack of adequate refrigeration, and in the storage facilities of the Ministry of fruit and vegetables. On the second page there was a large article about losses of milk. The same topic, quoting examples of losses of other dairy products, was the subject of a letter-article written by a group of farmers, on page 3.[2] The change of tone in the press was unmistakable, and the message was clear: if people want to eat better, they will have to work harder.

There were more ominous signs of a tougher policy towards workers and farmers as soon as the December celebrations of the sixtieth anniversary of the foundation of the USSR were over. The papers continued to campaign for an increase in labour discipline and an improvement in work ethics; meanwhile the police and other organs of control began a real offensive against all forms of un-registered freelance work, 'moonlighting' or the 'second economy'. There are certainly cases where the 'second economy' in the Soviet Union is closely linked with official corruption, but in general the workers who do private repairs of apartments, plumbing, electrical goods, etc. badly need their extra income because of their low official sal-aries. Moreover, they fill a void in the state-provided services. As a rule, people simply cannot get their cars repaired quickly and reliably in state garages; they have to wait years to get their state-owned apartments repaired (and even then the work is likely to be very shoddy indeed); and they cannot get help to build small sheds on their officially permitted 'garden allotments". In provincial towns the in-adequacy of all services is even more evident than in the cities, and private, unregistered work fills the gap. Even factories and collective farms often use unofficial labour to repair equipment. It was premature to crack down on this 'second economy', and this was the first serious mistake of the new leadership. The idea that if workers are prevented from doing freelance work they will start working harder in their factories so as to earn more through overtime and by exceeding their quotas is misguided and simplistic. Stalin tried this approach in agriculture in 1949–52 and failed. Khrushchev got better results with his economic reforms in 1953–58, but when he started to apply administrative measures and various kinds of pressure to restrict private agriculture (in 1960–64), so that peasants would devote more effort to their kolkhozes, he harmed both private and collective agriculture. Work discipline is poor not only because of a lack of administrative zeal but also because of low salaries: the average worker's pay of 150 roubles per month (£100) does not provide sufficient incentive. Denying people the opportunity of earning extra money in the 'second economy' is unlikely to make them work harder for their inadequate salaries in the 'first' one.

The measures taken by the Soviet government at the beginning of 1983 bore less resemblance to the Hungarian model than to the example of martial law in Poland. As in Poland, the government decided to increase food prices, at first by the less obvious technique of rapidly expanding co-operative, or so-called 'commercial' trde. Co-operative shops function midway between the free collective farm markets and official state shops, and this is reflected in the prices they charge. People who cannot find heavily subsidized food in the ordinary state shops or who cannot spare the many hours required to queue, can buy better-quality food in co-operative shops. But since the distribution and production systems which run these shops are not subsidized, prices are double or treble those in the ordinary state shops. More and more food has been diverted into this system, and newspaper articles are appearing to explain its pricing policies to worried consumers.[3] These measures have increased the total amount that the population pays for food and are probably the first step in a policy to increase food prices in general. The government is engaged in an active campaign to convince the public that the prices for bread and other essentials – prices which have remained unchanged for thirty years – are too low. While it is difficult, in economic terms, to argue against the view that food is too heavily subsidized in the Soviet Union, to accompany price rises with a crackdown on extra sources of income is hardly likely to reduce the general discontent which was a prevalent feature of the last years of Brezhnev's rule. Moreover, this combination of measures is unlikely to improve the general performance of the Soviet economy.

Andropov's well-publicized meeting with the workers and engineers of a Moscow machine-tool plant on 31 January 1983 was reported in all Soviet newspapers on 1 February. He again insisted on the need for better discipline, a stricter observance of the plan and a reduction in the loss of working time through absenteeism, slow work, breaks for cigarettes, etc. He disclosed no plans for economic reform, apart from hinting that the Soviet pricing system is imperfect and that some price increases are necessary.

Stricter discipline in rural areas has also been recommended. Meetings of state and collective farmers have been called to discuss ways of improving discipline and to threaten offenders with fines and administrative and legal measures. This may be the simplest and cheapest method to stem the decline in productivity in the short term, but it is unlikely to work in the long run without proper economic incentives. Such measures are acceptable only if they are temporary, designed to gain time so that real economic reforms can be developed and tested and so that bureaucrats can be replaced by genuine experts. But if stricter discipline backed up by administrative pressure is seen as the only cure for the ailing Soviet economy, positive results can hardly be expected.

14

The Drive against Corruption

In September 1980, under the influence of the collapse of the Gierek government in Poland, the Central Committee passed a resolution concerning measures to be taken against corruption in official circles which was distributed to regional and district Party organizations in the form of a secret Party circular. It was never published. This indicates that the Central Committee did not want to launch an open campaign or to introduce legal measures, which would have been the only way of making the new policy effective. The top leadership clearly realized how widespread the trouble was and how sensitive an issue, and hoped to improve the situation without causing serious embarrassment. However, in many Union and Autonomous Republics and in many regions the most serious violations of the socialist principle of the distribution of wealth according to work often occurred at the top level. Lower-level officials simply followed the example of higher officials or were sometimes included in a network of corruption which their superiors covered over and protected. Sometimes the illegal activity took the form of a well-organized business in the style of the mafia; in other cases there was a blatant misuse of state funds, property and labour for personal needs. There were several well-developed large-scale networks for smuggling certain items abroad (Soviet luxury exports like icons, furs, caviar and vodka) and then purchasing and smuggling back popular foreign goods (hi-fi equipment, jeans, sheepskin coats, etc.). Indeed, a striking feature of Soviet cities since the late 1970s has been the fact that people there look indistinguishable from people in London, Paris or any other European capital in spite of the fact that Western consumer goods and clothes are not on sale to the public.

The investigation of corrupt officials and economic crime and the initiation of legal action can be undertaken by several agencies in the Soviet Union: by the police and police investigators; by the public procurators' offices which have their own corps of investigators; and the KGB. In the West it is widely believed that the KGB is the most important of these. In fact the KGB is the body which deals with political dissent and serious state crimes such as treason and espionage, and it has very little to do with the investigation of corruption or economic offences. It becomes involved only if there is suspicion that the offences involve foreigners or foreign contacts, or high officials who have access to state secrets, or if they entail violence between different national groups. There is also a separate system of military investigators and courts for the armed forces. However, certain economic crimes cannot easily be detected or investigated by any of the bodies mentioned above. If, for example, the director or other officials of a large factory or industrial complex, which is not locally controlled but is part of a larger industrial grouping subordinate to an All-Union Ministry, are suspected of misappropriating building materials or part of the product, or in any other way misusing funds, the investigation will require the study of documents held in the offices of the Moscow Ministry. (There are three kinds of Ministries in the Soviet Union: All-Union Ministries are located in Moscow and have jurisdiction throughout the USSR; Union Republican Ministries have counterparts in the constituent Union Republics as well as a central Ministry in Moscow; Republican Ministries exist at the local, Union Republican level only.) Prosecution of the inquiry will also demand a financial expertise which neither the local police nor the KGB at central or local level are likely to have at their disposal. There are, therefore, specialized units in the Ministry of Internal Affairs and in the office of the General Procurator of the Soviet Union (and in the ministerial offices in the Union Republics) to deal with affairs of this nature. The best known is the 'Department for combating the embezzlement of socialist property' (*otdel po bor'be s khishcheniyami sotsialisticheskoi sobstvennosti*, or OBKSS) which has a great deal of experience and employs well-briefed detectives. In addition to all these agencies, the Ministry of Finance and other Ministries have special financial commissions which are required from time to time to conduct an audit of state organizations of all types from the smallest barber's shop to the largest industrial complex.

Despite so many formidable arrangements to combat economic crime, corruption is so widespread that practically every citizen is acquainted with it in one form or another and can provide examples from personal experience. One of the main problems in dealing with corruption is the difficulty of distinguishing between its 'legal' and 'illegal' manifestations. Stalin, for example, institutionalized a system of secret payments of large sums of money to all high officials, from the rank of obkom Party secretary upwards, in addition to their official salaries. The banknotes were delivered in special envelopes, and these monthly payments were supposed to be confidential – the recipient was expected not to tell anyone else about them. Were they a kind of bribe? The idea behind them was to prevent individuals becoming dependent upon the usual type of bribe or other illegal sources of income, since the average salary was not sufficient to support a reasonably good standard of living and it was taken for granted that people would be open to bribery. The payments were clearly against the law. On the other hand, they had been introduced by the government as an 'extraordinary measure' during the war, and retained after it. Khrushchev abolished them in 1956, but he soon introduced additional payments in kind, through a system of special shops and distributors where high officials could purchase items, or order them for delivery, at a very low cost or entirely free of charge. Khrushchev's intention was to save the valuable time of officials which would otherwise be wasted queuing, shopping and waiting around. Soon, however, the number of fringe benefits began to grow rapidly.

High Party officials became entitled to a free country cottage (dacha) – to at least two, if they were important enough, one close to their apartment for weekends and the other in a resort area like the Crimea, Sochi, Georgia or the North Caucasus. For each member of the Politburo there was an official residence in Moscow (dozens of houses were built on the Lenin Hills overlooking the Moscow river), although theoretically these were government property and the Politburo members retained their own private flats. The official residences were provided with salaried personnel: guards, waiters, cooks, maids, secretaries, etc. In Brezhnev's time 'maids', 'cooks' and 'secretaries' were sometimes euphemisms for high-class call-girls, employed for the pleasure of the Party dignitary himself or for his guests. The dachas became more and more palatial in style, with swimming-pools and tennis courts, all built at the expense of the state. In addition, Brezhnev gave every high official the right to have a specially stocked hunting forest, guarded and banned to ordinary hunters, near Moscow or else-where. In Borovsk, for example, sixty miles from Moscow, where I worked from 1970 to 1972, one of the good local forests of about 300 acres became a hunting area for the Politburo member D. S. Polyansky. 'Wild animals' were brought there from other parts of the Soviet Union. All these privileges became institutionalized, 'legal', and many more could be added to the list. It is small wonder, therefore, that other officials who received fewer 'fringe benefits' tried, nonetheless, to increase the luxury of their life-styles in every possible way, often exceeding the boundaries of legality. In any case the dividing line between the legal and the illegal was indistinct.

The kind of official corruption against which the 1980 campaign was directed was the excessively luxurious standard of living enjoyed by some high Party functionaries and the flagrantly illegal activity in which other highly placed people were involved. Two dramatic cases, which reached the dimensions of a national scandal, will serve to illustrate the magnitude of the problem and the high level at which corruption of this type occurred.

While large dachas were legitimate, for some officials this was not enough, and what they wanted in addition depended upon their taste, education and pastimes. Some 'borrowed' classical paintings from the reserves of local museums. One notorious scandal may, at the time of writing, still cost Grigorii Romanov his position as a member of the Politburo. Romanov replaced Tolstikov as First Secretary of the Leningrad obkom in 1970; he has a good war record and has served the Party well. However, he also has lavish tastes and in 1979, desiring to celebrate his daughter's wedding party with regal spendour, he ordered Catherine the Great's dinner service to be brought to his dacha from the Hermitage Museum. The service included hundreds of priceless, individually-made items, and all were used for the wedding dinner of Romanov's daughter. The whole affair might have gone unnoticed had intoxicated wedding guests not begun to follow tradition and to smash the royal glasses. Romanov could not, therefore, return the collection intact. How much damage was done is not known, for, of course, the incident was not treated as a crime. There was not even an investigation at the time.

The 'Great Caviar Scandal' uncovered in 1979 had continued for more than a decade and provided hundreds of officials with millions of roubles and hard currency. In 1980 details were published in several Western newspapers and magazines.[1] A criminal ring operated from Astrakhan on the Caspian Sea, involving the captains of several fishing boats and the workers in a caviar-packing plant, which hid a secret operation packing Russian black caviar in three-kilo

tins marked 'herring'. These tins of 'herring' were distributed to specially selected restaurants in Sochi and other
places, and shipped abroad where they were repacked in
small caviar tins and sold as caviar through accomplices in
the Soviet foreign trade network. In the restaurants the tins
were recorded as herring, but they were sold as caviar and
the extra cash was not registered. The Ministry of Fisheries
participated actively in the fraud: the Minister, Aleksandr
Ishkov, was partly involved and his deputy was at the head
of the syndicate. The whole illegal operation was discovered
by accident – some 'herring' tins were mistakenly dis-
patched for general sale and sold as herring in the Moscow
fish store 'Okean', where one customer, a police detective,
realized that they could be part of a fraud. Ishkov retired
immediately (he was seventy-three and an old friend of
Kosygin), his deputy was later sentenced to death and other
members of the ring received prison sentences. The Chairman of the Sochi City Council, V. A. Voronkov, who was
closely involved in the affair and was responsible for the
foreign bank account of the organization, was sentenced to
fourteen years. He only escaped the death sentence because
he co-operated closely with the joint KGB and OBKSS investigation, returning money from his foreign account and
naming some high officials in Moscow who were also part
of the ring.

However the Krasnodar obkom secretary, S. F. Medunov,
who was also implicated (Sochi and the other Black Sea
towns where people were arrested are in the Krasnodar *krai,*
or area), was protected from investigation. The General
Procurator's office accumulated evidence which showed
that Medunov's deputy was closely involved, but Medunov
would not allow the local KGB office to search his deputy's
apartment, and Brezhnev personally interfered to prevent
the continuation of the investigation of Medunov himself,
his old friend. The General Procurator's deputy who had
signed the search warrant was forced to resign. The trial
began in the summer of 1982, by which time Medunov's

deputy had been arrested, on other counts as well as the caviar case. Many other officials in Krasnodar were also arrested. Medunov himself was first transferred to another job, but by November 1982 he too was under house arrest. The case involving him was postponed in January 1983; his political life is certainly over, but unqualified exposure of a high Party official requires a consensus in the Politburo, and it is possible that the affair will be quietly shelved.

On a less dramatic scale, corruption exists in almost every office involved in arranging foreign trips, emigration, customs inspections, etc. I remember, for instance, that my professors in the Timiriazev Academy who were allowed to travel abroad had to bring special gifts to the head of the foreign department of the Ministry of Agriculture. The Chairman of the Moscow OVIR (the emigration department), Konstantin Zotov, was known for years as a man who took bribes from Jews for their exit permits (up to £2,000 in roubles), and members of his staff used to do the same. In the general situation of increased KGB power after Suslov's death and the suicide of Tsvigun, Zotov was arrested and about eighteen other OVIR officials in Moscow were also charged – OVIR was closed in March 1982 for a few weeks until new officials could be appointed. Like many other cases in which high functionaries were arrested, none of this was reported in the Soviet press, but it could not be kept secret from Moscow's Jewish community and reports appeared in the Jewish press abroad.[2]

After Brezhnev's death some reports about corruption at high levels began to appear in Soviet newspapers. On 18 December 1982 the penalties for corruption, embezzlement and bribery were increased. The new decree came into force on 1 January 1983.

In order to make clear who was behind the new anti-corruption drive, the Soviet newspapers published an unusual report, 'In the Politburo of the Central Committee of the CPSU', on 11 December 1982. This report showed that at its meeting the Politburo had discussed numerous letters from

workers and farmers complaining about shoddy work, falsi-
fication of statistics, uneconomic use of materials, arbitrari-
ness in the distribution of housing facilities, embezzlement of
funds and other violations of legality and justice. The report
stated that

> The Politburo drew the attention of the Procurator General
> of the USSR and the Ministry of Internal Affairs to the fact
> that it is necessary to take proper measures to improve social-
> ist legality in towns and villages, taking into consideration the
> fact that these problems are very frequently the cause of
> complaints in letters which are sent to the central Party
> organizations.[3]

An account of this Politburo meeting and its recommendations, published in all newspapers (which is itself unusual –
under Brezhnev, Politburo meetings were never reported),
indicated not only that Andropov was intent on stepping up
the anti-corruption campaign and making it serious – which
could have been predicted from the events before Brezhnev's
death – but also that many people, detecting a new trend in
his first speech in November, believed that it was a good time
to send in complaints about local problems. This is a common phenomenon in the USSR. When Stalin died and a few
weeks later the Government announced that the 'Doctors'
Plot' was a fabrication of some corrupt and criminal security
officials, millions of letters poured into the Central Committee, to Khrushchev and to Beria. After the arrest of Beria
and his closest associates, practically all the relatives of those
who were in the camps began to bombard the Central Committee with letters, petitions and appeals, demanding
rehabilitation whether or not their relatives were still alive. As
a personal instance, my father was arrested during the purges
in 1938 and died in an Arctic labour camp a few years later.
Although we knew he was dead, I, my mother and my
brother Roy began to send letters demanding his rehabilitation in 1953. He was rehabilitated in 1956. When one thinks

of the number of the victims of the purges and the size of the Gulag in 1953, it is clear that the Central Committee was suddenly deluged with appeals. Thousands of letters can be ignored, but when many millions start to arrive they must make a certain impact. Khrushchev was a bold man, and the rehabilitation of some of the victims of Stalin's terror must in large part be credited to him and to his decisive speech at the Twentieth Party Congress in 1956. But the uninterrupted flood of more and more insistent letters sent, over three years, to him, to the Central Committee, to the Government, to the General Procurator and to all other possible and impossible state and Party officials (added to the millions of letters from those who were still in the camps: the Gulag population in 1953 was about 23 million) must also have had a very important influence. It was clear that Khrushchev (who was himself guilty of participation in the terror) could not ignore the issue and that he could even use it to increase his popularity in the country.

After Brezhnev's death and Andropov's first hints about the Party line against corruption, the number of letters detailing various complaints sent to the Politburo, to the Central Committee and to other organizations apparently jumped to millions. Again it was a flood which neither Andropov nor his close associates could ignore. Corruption at all levels had become so widespread that the general public had come to believe that the shortages of food and consumer goods were in fact created by officials who took the lion's share of high-quality items through their closed shops, closed distribution networks and personal connections, leaving ordinary people with bread alone. Visitors to Moscow from provincial towns and villages could see how well dressed (and in *foreign* clothes), Moscow people were. They saw goods in Moscow which had not been available in their own towns for years.

This is why the new initiative against corruption cannot be explained entirely as emanating from the top. It was also the result of great pressure from below, expressed in the letters: the same kind of force which brought Solidarity to life in

Poland so quickly in August 1980 and made the organization ten million strong. In the Soviet Union mass dissatisfaction cannot yet find expression in such an open form. However, its leaders were forced to take serious notice of the public mood and public expectations.

15

Changes in Domestic Policies

Various social and national groups within the population inevitably expect particular measures to improve their situation when there is a change of leadership. But the preparation of reforms requires time and caution. Changes in the top leadership have taken place so infrequently in the USSR that people regard each one almost as if it were a revolution. Brezhnev was in power for eighteen years, which means that approximately half the active population today, i.e. all those between the ages of eighteen and thirty-eight, have either grown up or spent all their adult lives in the 'Brezhnev era'. They remember neither Stalinism nor the Khrushchev period: Andropov's accession is the first change of power which they have consciously witnessed.

Everyone is aware of the fact that many political and economic reforms are needed in the USSR, and this explains why so few people were enthusiastic about the possible accession of Konstantin Chernenko. The inevitability of a change of leadership had been clear for a long time, for television had made it obvious to everyone that the General Secretary was failing rapidly. Equally, the fact that Brezhnev had demonstrably chosen none other than Chernenko as his successor did not pass unnoticed. Although Chernenko had tried to make himself out to be a liberal, everyone knew that he would be no more than Brezhnev's ghost. Thus, despite a certain apprehension at the thought of being ruled by the former head of the KGB, there was a certain relief when Andropov was elected as General Secretary.

There were many rumours about the reforms which Andropov would introduce, and everyone waited impatiently for his major speech at the meeting of the Supreme Soviet held in December to celebrate the sixtieth anniversary of the foundation of the USSR. The whole of 1982 had been a jubilee year: the newspapers reminded readers of this every day from January onwards, running front-page articles and special jubilee features. A commemorative 'socialist competition' was declared in all branches of industry and agriculture in honour of the anniversary, and each day a list of workers who were leading in the competition, one from each republic, was published together with small photographs. The intention was to encourage others to step up productivity. However the campaign had little effect. Whether in terms of labour productivity, the growth of industry or the growth of the economy as a whole, 1982 was the worst year in the entire history of the USSR, with a growth rate of only 2.8 per cent. The 1982 plan, which had envisaged a 4 per cent growth in the economy, was far from being fulfilled. In 1981 industrial production had risen by 3.4 per cent, while even in agricultural production 1982 was only 4 per cent above 1981, a year of disastrous harvests. (The 1981–82 figures for grain production were not published in the annual statistical records, apparently because they were embarrassingly lower than in 1977–78.) In his speech to the Plenum of the Central Committee of the CPSU in November, Andropov criticized both industry and agriculture, but out of consideration for the jubilee, his tone was moderate and he concentrated on only a few branches of the economy.

In his sixtieth anniversary speech, Andropov was expected to present a new assessment of the various stages of development in the history of the USSR and to draw some general political conclusions. It would be an ideal opportunity for appraising the past and pointing the way to the future, and everyone was sure that he would make the most of it. His speech, therefore, was eagerly anticipated.

In the event, people's expectations were disappointed. The speech, broadcast on the radio on 21 December and published in all Soviet newspapers the following day, was unexpectedly short, lasting only about an hour. Andropov made no reference to historical questions. He did not mention Stalin or Khrushchev, and Brezhnev's name was mentioned only once. This unexpected failure to analyse the history of the Soviet system could be interpreted in various ways. It may have symbolized an intention to maintain silence about the acute problems of the past, a silence which so impeded the development of social thought during the 'Brezhnev era'. On the other hand, it could simply have meant that a new policy had not yet been worked out and that there was still no unanimity in the Politburo or the Central Committee about the need for reassessment, for a new approach to the analysis of the Soviet past.

Andropov singled out two issues in his speech: the problem of national minorities and the problem of peace. I shall discuss his pronouncements on foreign policy in the next section. The fact that he concentrated on the problem of nationalities is not accidental, for in spite of official assurances over many years that it has been resolved, this is by no means the case. It has frequently been noted that national conflict has increased over the last few years, and this conflict forms the basis of the many predictions that the 'Soviet empire' will, inevitably, disintegrate. National dissension has been the subject of scholarly studies[1] as well as individual comments by foreign leaders, some of them as experienced as Henry Kissinger.[2] Although the Western press exaggerates the possible political repercussions of these conflicts, the problems themselves are very real. It is a well-known fact, for example, that the birthrate in the Soviet Central Asian republics is much higher than in Russian, Ukrainian and Byelorussian ones. As a result, the national groups of Soviet Central Asia are fast increasing their proportion among the general population, while their migration to other parts of the country has been minimal. This causes the acute problem of an excess labour force in some national areas. The percentage of industrial workers in the population is highest in Latvia and Estonia (16.6 and 16.3 per cent) and the Russian Federation (15.5 per cent). It is extremely low in Turkmenia, Uzbekistan and Tadzhikistan (4.1–4.4 per cent). Thus the labour reserves are in the Moslem areas of the country, and migration within the Soviet Union must be stimulated. However, the Moslem population is conservative about migration, and conditions will have to be improved to encourage them. Almost all the new industrial developments in Siberia, for example, depended on the migration of workers from the European parts of the Soviet Union, not from Central Asia.

The movement of the labour force has created particular grounds for discontent, and the charge of Russification has been laid. While the Russian language can be studied throughout the country, the Georgian and Tadzhik languages, to give two examples, are taught only in Georgia or Tadzhikistan respectively. The children of a Georgian or Tadzhik family which has moved to Moscow, Riga, Novosibrisk or Krasnoyarsk for employment cannot continue their education in their native language since the local schools do not have the necessary facilities. A Tadzhik in Novosibirsk not only cannot find a school for his children where Tadzhik is taught; there are also no Tadzhiks in managerial positions or in the local Party leadership who would be able to understand his problems. Thus, for some nationalities, moving to another republic is tantamount to emigrating abroad. The situation has created severe political problems and has also had economic consequences. The mobility of the work force is adversely affected, since people are reluctant to move, and this in turn slows down the economic development of the country. The Donbas in the Ukraine, centre of the coal-mining industry for a hundred years, has been worked out, and it would be logical to move hundreds of thousands of the miners there, many of them from traditional mining families, to new coalfields in Siberia. But no Ukrainian is spoken in Siberia, and Russification would be unavoidable. Similarly, the time has come to move qualified oil workers from the oil fields of Azerbaijan and Bashkiriya to the oil fields of Siberia. But oil workers often prefer to change their profession in order to remain in their own republics.

Of course Andropov did not speak directly or openly about these problems. Soviet speeches, whether on ordinary occasions or on jubilees, are not normally platforms for really sharp criticism. But in an oblique way he admitted that there were shortcomings in the nationalities policy. He particularly emphasized the need to promote national cadres to leading positions in republics other than their own, and called for the representation of various nationalities in the leading bodies of both the USSR and the constituent republics (since both the USSR and the Union Republics are multinational). This important proposal passed unnoticed in the foreign press, but it was certainly noted within the USSR. Although there is a tradition within the Party that the First Secretaries of the Union Republics are members of the Central Committee of the CPSU, and the First Secretaries of the Autonomous Republics and regions are members of the Republican Central Committees, it is clear that the principle of national equality is, at present, ignored in the executive organs. Practically all the Ministers of the USSR are Russian (with the exception of a small number of Ukrainians and Byelorussians). The idea of a Tadzhik Minister is alsmost unthinkable. In Georgia about 30 per cent of the population is Armenian and 10 per cent Caucasian Moslem (Abkhazians and Adzharians), but the government of Georgia is composed of Georgians (with a few Russians). The same is true at the regional level: in large regions such as Chelyabinsk, Sverdlovsk or Krasnoyarsk the Party and state leadership is almost 100 per cent Russian. Not surprisingly, the national minorities perceive this as discrimination. Perhaps Andropov's new policy directive will change the situation. In the long term, the aim is to make internal migration of the population easier, which will help to promote assimilation and reduce national barriers.

Andropov's speech was the only interesting item in the sixtieth anniversary celebrations. The other speeches made at the session of the Supreme Soviet were as boring and formal as usual. The long-established ritual of dreary cliché remained undisturbed.

The next eagerly anticipated event was the declaration of an amnesty, again in honour of the sixtieth anniversary of the USSR. This would be a more important index of change than the anniversary speeches, and both Soviet people and Western observers had high hopes. Alexander Solzhenitsyn's repeated insistence that there has never been a political amnesty in the Soviet Union is not quite true. Khrushchev declared an important political amnesty in 1955, in connection with the establishment of diplomatic relations with West Germany and the visit of Chancellor Adenauer to Moscow, when he freed all those who had been accused of collaborating with the Germans in occupied territory, except for those who had fought with the German army or served in the German police. Those who had merely co-operated in order to survive, like village elders, interpreters, people who had worked in the civil service of the occupying administration, were released. In 1956 there was a second amnesty. Thousands of concentration camps were closed down and millions of the victims of Stalin's purges were rehabilitated, while those who could not be rehabilitated because the relevant facts were unavailable were granted an amnesty. In the 'Brezhnev era' there were relatively few political prisoners, but no political amnesties. Now many people hoped that Andropov would extend his amnesty to political prisoners – perhaps not to all of them, but at least to some groups, such as those who had not committed 'particularly dangerous state crimes'. (I have already mentioned that, in 1966, when it became apparent that Article 70 of the Criminal Code, which puts all political 'crimes' into the category of 'very dangerous', made it difficult to deal with dissidents, the Supreme Soviet adopted

Article 190–1, which had made it possible to convict people for political offences even when there was no intention to overthrow the Soviet system. Offences of this kind were now classified in the highly dubious category of 'Crimes against the administrative order', which allowed for a maximum penalty of three years' imprisonment.) Even Western observers expected there to be an extensive amnesty. *Newsweek* commented:

> Some prisoners in the Soviet Union may have good reason to celebrate Dec. 30 – the 60th anniversary of the founding of the U.S.S.R. It is a Soviet tradition to grant amnesty to some criminal – though not political – prisoners on major anniversaries. A number of Kremlin watchers in Moscow believe that new Communist Party leader Yuri Andropov will proclaim an unusually generous amnesty; they reason that the former KGB chief will be eager to demonstrate that he knows the difference between administering the state and running the secret police.[3]

Unfortunately none of these expectations were fulfilled. The amnesty decree of the Presidium of the Supreme Soviet dated 27 December 1982 was as selective as the 1972 decree had been, and included no political prisoners. 'Guided by the principles of socialist humanity', the amnesty released a few categories of prisoners who had been sentenced for periods of up to five years, such as war veterans, medalholders, and women. Certain special groups of people serving longer sentences were also freed: men over the age of sixty (who were too old to work productively in the camps anyway), pregnant women, invalids, etc.[4] The amnesty did not include anyone who had been convicted for 'particularly dangerous crimes against the state', and this, of course, excluded people like Yuri Orlov, Sergei Kovalev and other well-known members of the Helsinki group who had been sentenced under Article 70. But some non-state crimes were also specified as being outside its provision, including offences under Article 190–1, 'The deliberate dissemina-

tion of slanderous information which defames the Soviet
state and social order'. Thus the amnesty did not apply to
dissidents, writers or other protesters. Religious dissidents
convicted under Articles 142 and 227, 'Breaking the laws on
the separation of the church from the state and schools from
the church' – i.e. those who wanted to give their children a
religious education – were also excluded. Even that rare and
insignificant political offence, 'Violating the state coat of
arms or flag', punishable by a fine or imprisonment for up to
two years under Article 190–2, was not covered by the
amnesty. Article 190–3, 'The organization of or active
participation in group activities which disturb the public
order', used against those who have tried to organize small
protest demonstrations, also remained outside its scope.

Thus the amnesty hardly turned out to be the 'unusually
generous' event predicted by *Newsweek* and hoped for in
the Soviet Union. Of course, any amnesty is a good thing,
and one may rejoice for all those pregnant women and
young people who, out of carelessness or a jolly evening of
drinking, ended up in prison. (Soviet law is very severe, and
comparatively minor infringements are classed as 'hooliganism' and punished by sentences of between three and
seven years. Many adolescents end up in camps because of
'hooliganism'.) Perhaps 500,000 of the three million people
in corrective labour camps will be released (though the
number will never be publicly announced). Political and
religious dissidents at present form an insignificant proportion of the camp population – there are a few thousand
in all, far less than 1 per cent. Their release would present no
danger to the state and would be perceived abroad as a
genuinely humane act. It is regrettable that the new leadership has missed this opportunity.

Clearly the corrective labour camps will soon fill up again,
as the campaign against petty crime gains momentum. This
campaign is part of a more alarming sign of mounting
internal control. At the beginning of January 1983 an unprecedented round-up of people who were 'infringing

labour discipline' began, code-named *Tral* (Trawl). Because of inadequacies in the supply of food, particularly to the provinces, many provincial residents travel to Moscow to shop; and since most stores have a better selection available during normal working hours than on weekends or in the evenings, both Muscovites and people from other towns take time off from work to do their shopping. Suddenly, at the beginning of January, the militia began to take an interest in any queue outside a shop. A police bus would load up with people from the queue and take them to the nearest police station to establish their identity. The manager, or Party office, was informed of anyone who was playing truant from work, so that the offence could be noted and an appropriate deduction made from the person's salary. Those who could not produce their documents remained at the police station for even longer. As a result, people now carry their identity documents around at all times, and visitors to Moscow from the provinces are required to have a certificate to prove that they have been given the day off or are on leave. There have even been daytime raids on the public baths in Moscow, where Muscovites love to spend their time, drinking beer after a traditional steam bath. The round-ups are directed towards increasing labour discipline and eliminating petty crime, particularly in the provinces, and have also had an effect on the 'black market' – it has long been known to the militia where various 'black market' deals are concluded, and such places have been raided. Thus the camps, slightly emptier after the December amnesty, were probably full again by the end of January. It was not, in any case, in the interests of the authorities to allow them to become too depleted. Every labour camp in the Soviet Union is attached to a particular factory, so that a reduced prison population would cause a setback in the production plan for the corrective labour system. To illustrate this, in 1971, when my eighteen-year-old son was convicted of hooliganism, he was first sent to a 'mild regime' camp in which the prisoners built roads.

Security at this camp was lax and my son decided to escape. He was caught after three weeks of travelling around and this time he was sent to a strict regime camp in Kaluga. However, his luck held out, for this camp was attached to a furniture factory and, as a result, he was taught a useful trade. Usually, though, the camps are affiliated to less attractive industries, particularly those which have difficulty recruiting labour from the free labour market.

Various sections of the intelligentsia have been expecting a shift in the policy towards literature, art and science. Whereas Brezhnev took practically no interest in these problems, entrusting them to Suslov, Andropov clearly wants to keep up the reputation of being an intellectual which he acquired when he worked in the Central Committee apparatus. Even when he was head of the KGB, in conversations with artists or scientists he would claim to be speaking as a member of the Politburo rather than as KGB chairman, hinting that he was merely the political boss of the KGB and not the person who controlled its current operations. After he was elected to the post of General Secretary, he summoned the President of the Academy of Sciences, Anatolii Aleksandrov, to see him on several occasions. While the subject-matter of their talks is not known, Georgii Markov, Chairman of the Union of Soviet Writers, told a meeting of Moscow writers in January about his own conversation with Andropov about the role of literature and the cinema. Andropov's advice was not received with much enthusiasm, for he criticized the late Yuri Trifonov, an extremely popular writer, for being too interested in the problems of daily life. While he admitted that talented authors should be allowed a degree of freedom of choice of attitude and subject-matter, at the same time he argued that literature had the duty to help the Party and state in its struggle for order. These are ancient slogans, and unlikely to encourage the Soviet intelligentsia.

The thousands of people who have applied to emigrate must also have been wondering whether Andropov will introduce a change of policy. After the peak in 1979, when more than 50,000 people left the Soviet Union, emigration has fallen to the 1970 level, and in 1982 only 2,692 people were allowed to leave (about 4 per cent of the 1979 level). I doubt whether there will be any significant change in the immediate future. Emigration policy has come to reflect international events and is now a barometer of relations between the Soviet Union and the USA. Israel's intervention in the Lebanon has made Jewish emigration more difficult, and there has been little improvement in Soviet–American relations. The immediate prospects for those who are waiting to leave do not seem hopeful. According to the international Jewish organizations which monitor the Jewish emigration rate, of the 2,692 people who left in 1982, the lowest monthly rate was in December, when only 176 people received permission to leave. The ban on private teaching of Hebrew also continued through December and January.

Andropov's pronouncements on literature, the curb on emigration and the very limited nature of the amnesty make it clear that the few remaining dissidents can have little cause for optimism. One of the leaders of the Soviet human rights movement, the former General Petro Grigorenko, who now lives in New York, predicted that Andropov would make a few liberal gestures to reassure the West, such as, allowing Academician Andrei Sakharov to return to Moscow from his exile in Gorky. Nothing of the kind has happened. Given the general trend of the drive against corruption and crime and the disciplinary approach to both blue- and white-collar workers, it is extremely unlikely that dissidents will gain greater freedom of action. It is far more probable that the last tiny vestiges of the democratic opposition will be eliminated. When officials are being arrested and when Ministers, including the Minister of Internal Affairs, are being removed, no-one in the West or in the USSR is going to pay much attention to an intensified persecution of dissidents. In the jubilee month of December everything was quiet, but by the beginning of 1983 a clearer trend began to emerge.

Georgii Vladimov, the author of a major novel published in the USSR in 1969, *Tri minuty molchaniya* (*Three Minutes of Silence*),[5] and of a number of other novels which have been published abroad, including *Faithful Ruslan*,[6] was called to the Procurator's Office at the beginning of January and told that he had been implicated in a case against two members of the anti-Soviet organization NTS (*Narodno-trudovoi soyuz*, The People's Labour Union), which has its headquarters in Munich. Several of Vladimov's books have been published by Posev, which is closely associated with the NTS. For a number of years he has been withstanding pressure by the authorities to force him to emigrate but he has now received an ultimatum – either leave, or stand trial. He has applied to emigrate, but the outcome of his case is still in doubt and the possibility of a trial cannot be excluded. The KGB prefers first to compromise fairly well-known people and only then to permit them to leave, so that their departure is perceived as an act of clemency.

In the middle of January 1983 my brother Roy was given a clear signal that his freedom to write has its limits. He was summoned by special delivery to present himself to the Deputy General Procurator of the USSR, Comrade Soroka, on Tuesday, 18 January, as I discovered when I telephoned him on 16 January. Roy does not normally inform foreign correspondents or even his friends about events like this because he considers that a summons to appear before the Procurator is a professional risk undertaken by any in-dependent writer in the USSR. This was not the first time the KGB had taken an interest in him: twice previously, in 1971 and 1976, his flat was searched and many books and archive material confiscated. He has also been 'warned' by local organs and visited by the local police, who have told him that he must arrange employment for himself (although no professional work has been offered him since 1971). In 1976 he was summoned to the Moscow Procurator and warned to stop writing 'anti-Soviet, slanderous libels'; it seemed possible that he would receive a similar warning this time, only from a higher level.

However, after this summons, my attempts to telephone Roy were unsuccessful: the Moscow operator informed the British one that his telephone was out of order. On the morning of 19 January his telephone was still disconnected, which could have meant that his flat was being searched (telephones are usually disconnected while this activity takes place). I was worried, and decided to telephone two journalists I know who live in Moscow, and several American and European newspapers which have published Roy's articles.

As a result, Western correspondents in Moscow went to Roy's flat on Wednesday, 19 January. It took a further day for the telephone to be reconnected and so my first information about what had happened at the Procurator's office came from Western newspapers. Robert Kaiser, one of the foreign editors of the *Washington Post* and their Moscow correspondent from 1972 to 1975, telephoned me from Washington on the evening of 19 January to read me the article which was to appear the next day. I reproduce it here in a shortened version:

Moscow, Jan. 19. Roy Medvedev, the Soviet historian known in the West for his study of Stalinism, has been formally warned that he must cease his 'anti-Soviet activities' or face criminal charges for damaging 'the interests of the Soviet state' . . .

. . . Medvedev was summoned yesterday to the office of the Soviet procurator general, the nation's top law enforcement officer, to be served with a written statement in which his books and articles were described as 'pamphlets' that 'slandered the Soviet social and political system.'

The 57-year-old Marxist historian, whose independent views and activities have made him a political anomaly here, said today he had categorically rejected the charge. In a written statement to the procurator general, Medvedev accused the investigator's office of 'crudely violating' the Soviet constitution ...

   ... In an interview today, Medvedev said Deputy Procurator General Oleg Soroka had told him that 'either you cease writing such articles and books or we shall put you in jail.' Medvedev also quoted Sorok as saying that this was a message from 'the leadership' which was urging the historian to 'engage in socially useful activities.'

   ... No specific complaints about his writings were mentioned, Medvedev said.

   ... Defending his position, Medvedev said in his statement that his only aim was to see his country living in peace and flourishing in socialism and democracy. But, he said, corruption and misuse of power in 'our recent past' had infiltrated the Kremlin leadership including the legal system, the procurator's office and the KGB secret police.

   'In a country such as the Soviet Union.' he said, 'any honourable historian' must pursue his work irrespective of whether it is pleasing to those in power. 'Therefore I am but little concerned what assessment of my work is made by the procurator's office or the KGB.'

   'Any honest and independent historian must be concerned only by one thing – the search for truth. I am not afraid of any potential punishment and therefore it does not make much sense to make any warnings on this account or to resort to undignified threats.'

   He concluded: 'I consider that the interference of your deputy in my work is unjust and illegal and I ask that in the future I be protected from such actions which are undertaken not for the first time.'[7]

I personally believe that the harsh new policy towards the few remaining political groups and independent writers in Moscow and other cities is part of a general campaign against all forms of disobedience, indiscipline and infringement of the law. The wording of Soviet laws makes it very difficult to distinguish between critical analysis of the present or the past, and anti-Soviet propaganda. And since the regime in power is by definition always right, any criticism affecting the interests of the authorities is automatically classed as 'slander' and comes under Articles 70 or 190–1 of the Criminal Code. In any case, it is not difficult to see why the authorities might consider the publication of uncensored books and articles abroad to be an 'infringement of discipline' or an 'anti-Soviet act'. It may well be that the leadership has decided that it is a good time, in the midst of a campaign against corruption and crime, to put a complete end to all forms of political and national opposition, having in mind the old adage, so well known in the Soviet Union: 'When you cut for timber, you lose some chips of wood' (or, perhaps more apt, 'You may as well be hanged for a sheep as for a lamb').

However, the new 'hard line' has, without doubt, been a mistake. It is not very far-sighted to begin one's rule with repression of the intelligentsia and acts of coercion against workers. Ordering a massive round-up of people queuing for food is a crude political error. Checking the documents of people going to the cinema in the middle of the day and sending a whole queue of people waiting at the box-office of a popular theatre to the police station is not only a crude mistake but a violation of the law. Perhaps the hand of Fedorchuk, the new MVD Minister, can be seen here. As a former KGB general, it may be that he is unaware of the fact that the approach and methods of the KGB are not appropriate in the MVD. The KGB, like the secret services of all countries, often breaks the law under the pretext of defending state security. But the militia must act within the law, if it is to uphold it. The massive round-up of people who are not at work when they should be and the identity-checks on people at public baths and in cinemas have done nothing to improve labour discipline. What they have done is to provoke general indignation. The Politburo began to receive thousands of letters complaining about the lawlessness of the police, and since one of its own reports in December promised a serious response to letters from workers, it was forced to reconsider its own tactics. As a result, the government indirectly admitted its own repsonsibility for the fact that people have to queue during working hours – after all, practically all food shops, and indeed services in general, are usually open only between 9 a.m. and 6 or 7 p.m. In a resolution of the Council of Ministers of the USSR of 17 January, the decision was taken to change the working hours of the trade network and of service sector organizations and to increase the number of shops, workshops, hairdressers, etc. which are 'on duty' in the evenings. It was further proposed that 'the opening times of enterprises, organizations, and institutions in the service sphere be re-examined so that they are more convenient for workers'.[8] By the end of January, the round-ups in Moscow and other cities were either no longer taking place or had become more selective. Clearly, the new leadership, whose main experience has been in the army and the KGB (Andropov, Ustinov and Aliyev in effect form the main 'triumvirate'), has something to learn about administrative work in a civilian environment. Aliyev may have had considerable success using strict disciplinarian control in Azerbaijan but an approach of this kind is clearly not suitable for Moscow or Leningrad.

Meanwhile the cases against several groups of dissidents have been prepared. These are a religious group, a small NTS group, and a few young Social Democrats including A. Fadin, P. Kudykin, and Y. Kagarlizky, who discussed ways of improving Soviet socialism, which they saw as undemocratic. The outcome of these trials will be an important indication of the political intentions of the new leadership.

16

New Trends in Foreign Policy

The new trends in Soviet foreign policy were immediately apparent: they began to emerge at the Kremlin reception after Brezhnev's funeral on 15 November 1982. The whole experience of the reception, with so many high-level foreign delegations present, was new to the Soviet leaders – it had never happened before. There were very few foreigners at Lenin's funeral in January 1924; more attended Stalin's more elaborate funeral, but most of these were from socialist countries. Moreover, the main objective of the new Soviet leadership after Stalin's death was to display enormous grief at their irreparable loss: nobody tried to do business at the reception afterwards. A few hours after Brezhnev's death and well before his funeral the leadership had resumed normal work, and the Kremlin reception was used as a unique opportunity for personal diplomacy. Nobody missed the signs that appeared there: Andropov's longer than usual and very friendly talk with the Chinese Foreign Minister, Huang Hua, and the encouraging remarks he made to President Zia of Pakistan. Later he met the American delegation headed by Vice-President Bush and some other delegations for talks, but these were brief and without any specifically prepared agenda. Even this, however, represented a new approach and, even more, a display of Andropov's flexibility and intelligence. Brezhnev would never have been able to engage in such spontaneous exchanges on a variety of issues – it would simply have been beyond his capabilities. Andropov managed, in the course of a single day, to make it absolutely clear to about one hundred foreign delegations that he was firmly in charge of foreign affairs and that they must expect changes. The period of diplomatic stagnation was over.

A new beginning in Sino–Soviet relations

It was already clear from Brezhnev's speeches in Tashkent in March and in Baku in September 1982 that the leadership had decided to try to improve relations between the Soviet Union and China. There had been earlier attempts when it had become clear in 1976 that Mao Tse-Tung's death was being followed by some kind of 'de-Maoization'. To the Chinese, Mao was the counterpart of both Lenin and Stalin, and therefore their new leaders had a more difficult task than Khrushchev was faced with in 1956–62. They had to leave the Leninist side of Mao intact, whilst destroying his Stalinist image; and they had to draw a line between the Leninism and the Stalinism in 'Maoism'. Mao's death had a profound effect on the world Communist movement as a whole. Many Communist Parties in the East were split in two, one pro-Soviet, the other pro-Chinese. Within two or three years this split disappeared, the Maoist factions in most of the Communist parties ceased to exist, while the number of Maoist groups among the 'New Left' in other countries also declined.

The continuation of a hostile attitude to the Soviet Union isolated the Chinese Communist Party from an ideological point of view. Friendly relations with the USA and other Western countries made a quarrel with Albania, China's only friend in the Communist world, inevitable. The pro-Chinese Pol Pot regime in Cambodia was so brutal and barbaric that it was more of an embarrassment than an asset. It was in this situation that the first signs – slight, but unmistakable – of a softening in the Chinese attitude to the Soviet Union began. Soviet citizens listening to broadcasts from China in Russian noticed that criticism of the Soviet system had become milder and that glorification of both Stalin and Mao had disappeared. The USSR was now said to be a socialist regime in the economic sense, albeit 'with hegemonic tendencies'. Chinese propaganda also stopped treating Soviet-style 'revisionism' as original sin – the Chinese leaders had themselves become extremely revisionist in their approach to the USA and other capitalist countries. There were still many problems to solve, but the process had begun.

The China–Vietnam conflict at the end of 1978 and beginning of 1979 (following the Vietnamese occupation of Kampuchea), which developed into a brief but intense military confrontation when China attempted to 'teach Vietnam a lesson', delayed the Sino–Soviet rapprochement. For some time there were even fears that the Soviet Union would intervene directly in the war, if the Chinese offensive began to threaten Hanoi. Fortunately, this did not happen. However, the new military dimension to the conflicts between Vietnam and Kampuchea and between China and Vietnam put the Soviet Union in a very difficult position and greatly contributed to the fatal decision made by the Brezhnev leadership to invade Afghanistan at the end of 1979. Afghanistan was a poor, semi-feudal country and nobody really expected it to become an American satellite if the Taraki–Amin regime collapsed. However, the fear was that it might become an ally of China, which could then form a tripartite alliance with Pakistan. The Soviet invasion of Afghanistan in 1979 was a pre-emptive strike to prevent this happening. This is a simplified version of a rather complex regional policy, but serves to illustrate the way in which Brezhnev was thinking. He was known to be virulently anti-Chinese, and was personally responsible for the ill-advised decision during the border conflict in 1969 to 'teach China a lesson'. It was Brezhnev who ordered the massive artillery attack against Chinese troops then, which resulted in the deaths of several thousand Chinese soldiers and a sense of deep injury in the Chinese attitude towards the

Soviet Union. It also made real rapprochement very difficult while Brezhnev remained in office.

There were many political and economic factors in 1981–82 that favoured new attempts to heal old wounds and to return at least to some kind of dialogue. The main reason, of course, was the Taiwan policy of the Reagan administration, which made it very difficult for Chinese propaganda to explain and justify the close tie with the USA. China's failure to achieve the promised rapid modernization on the basis of sophisticated Western (and Japanese) technology was a further factor. Chinese experiments with foreign loans and credits had been unsuccessful – the difficulties of repayment had proved to be formidable. Moreover, Chinese heavy industry had been built up on the basis of Soviet projects during the 1950s, and China badly needed to update and modernize its Soviet-designed plant and equipment. China has enormous reserves of cheap labour and does not really require sophisticated computerized Japanese technology. For full employment to be achieved, less sophisticated Soviet and Eastern European systems are probably more suitable, as well as being less expensive and easier to operate. There was thus nothing the USSR and China could gain from continuing hostile relations, while there was much to be gained from rapprochement. Although President Reagan's aggressive anti-Communist crusade was directed essentially against the Soviet Union, it affected China as well because of its ideological basis. China is, in every sense, a Communist country, and in Mao's time it prided itself upon being even more Communist than its 'revisionist' northern neighbour. Chinese leaders are not insensitive to the anti-Communist 'Cold War', even if it is not their own country which is being stigmatized.

The Soviet press carried fewer articles criticizing current or past aspects of Chinese policy, and included a number of more positive accounts of cultural, artistic and scientific developments in China. The Chinese dispute with Japan over the content of Japanese textbooks which, according to the Chinese, distorted the history of the last war was widely reported in Soviet newspapers. But political and historical criticism of China did not cease, in spite of Brezhnev's conciliatory statements, which were rather coolly received in China. Academic journals continued to publish articles detailing the errors and miscalculations of Chinese leaders and their policies of aggression. An excellent article by Fyodor Burlatskii published in the April 1982 issue of *Novy Mir*[1] attracted a great deal of attention among Soviet intellectuals – less, in fact, because of its criticism of the Chinese leadership than because its sophisticated political analysis was rare in Soviet scholarship, and because it could also be read as a parable of Soviet history.

It could be argued that it was Brezhnev himself who introduced the new policy towards China. There are signs, however, that it was in fact Andropov's policy, and his friendly chat with the Chinese foreign minister is not the only indication of this. It is possible that he initiated certain moves when he became Secretary in charge of ideology, and that the Chinese knew of this. By October–November 1982, articles critical of China had ceased to appear in the Soviet Union, and scholars who had written papers under the previous ideological regime and had submitted them for publication suddenly began to receive them back. To the initiated this meant that the Chinese were now considered to be in the same category as other socialist countries and that the censors had been instructed to this effect. Criticism of the leaders of friendly socialist states is forbidden in the Soviet press. In China, meanwhile, the publication of anti-Soviet literature continues, but the volume has been significantly reduced.

At the end of November 1982 a new 'Law on the Soviet State Border' was prepared and introduced to a session of the Supreme Soviet and became effective on 1 March 1983.[2] While a law of such magnitude (forty articles) must have been in preparation while Brezhnev was alive, the initiative for it belongs to Vitalii Fedorchuk, who introduced it to the

Supreme Soviet in his capacity as Chairman of the KGB. The
last border law was adopted in 1960.[3] The new law contains
new customs regulations, changes in the definition of the
powers of frontier patrols, etc. From the point of view of the
Sino–Soviet border dispute, it provides a comfortable and
face-saving formula for possible Soviet concessions. The
most serious part of the dispute concerned the 500-mile
stretch of border at the Ussuri River – according to an
agreement signed over a hundred years ago, the whole of
this river belongs to Russia and the border is on the Chinese
bank. This was unfair, of course, for both countries need the
river for transport, fishing and other purposes. The usual
practice when a border is along a river is to draw the line
either in the middle of the river or in the middle of the
navigation channel, so as to give both sides equal navigation
rights. In the European parts of the USSR, on the border
with Romania and other countries, this principle has been
respected. In the case of the Sino–Soviet border it was not
respected, and in the winter of 1969 there were clashes
between Soviet and Chinese soldiers over some small islands
which were on the Chinese side of the main river stream and
which, in all fairness, ought to belong to China.

Article 3 of the new law clearly stipulates that 'on rivers
suitable for transportation the border runs through the
middle of the navigation channel', and in the middle of the
waterway if the river is not fit for navigation. In previous
laws the same principle had been affirmed, but with reservations, indicating that it applied only if there were no previous
agreements about the border. The Soviet position on the
dispute with China has always been that the agreement
made in the nineteenth century between the Czarist government of the Russian Empire and Imperial China is still valid.
The Chinese position was more logical – they insisted that
the October Revolution nullified treaties signed by the
Czarist government and that a new agreement was necessary.
This has apparently been conceded. Article 2 of the new law
makes it plain that the state border can be determined only

by agreement between the USSR and other parties; the reservation about previous treaties is removed. This effectively invalidates the old Czarist treaty and lays this part of the border dispute open to settlement. China has other territorial claims which will prove more difficult to resolve, but, nonetheless in this particular case the Soviet Union has made a long overdue concession. It has been reported several times in the foreign press recently that tension in this border area has all but disappeared. A new stage of Sino–Soviet negotiations could probably reach a compromise about the other major Chinese demand, a reduction in the number of Soviet troops along the border, for if tension there had genuinely been reduced, the presence of about fifty Soviet divisions would become superfluous.

The problems of Afghanistan and Kampuchea, resolution of which the Chinese have made a precondition of improved relations, are more complex, but discussions about them could certainly begin. China is not completely innocent in either area, for without Chinese military and economic aid the Pol Pot forces would have been wiped out long ago, while in Afghanistan the Chinese have probably aggravated the intensity of the civil war. Economic difficulties in both China and the USSR (and in Vietnam) make it clear that a policy of confrontation is too costly, with each side paying too high a price and receiving little in return. Brezhnev suffered from 'Sinophobia', which he made no attempt to hide, even when talking to foreign visitors. It was certainly well known in Peking, and the only warm words the Chinese have ever said about Brezhnev were contained in their telegram of condolence after his death. The Chinese leaders find it much easier to deal with Andropov, and this disappearance of personal animosity will be an important factor in the future development of Sino–Soviet relations. However, even though the process of 'normalization' has accelerated after Brezhnev's death, it cannot be very rapid. Mutual hostility has been cultivated for so long that a real improvement will take some time. However, this is certainly an important new trend which could have a profound effect on other aspects of Soviet foreign policy.

The problem of Afghanistan

As head of the KGB Andropov must certainly have been a member of the special military strategic group which was given the task of planning the Afghanistan operation. It is quite possible, as reported in *Time* magazine on the basis of an interview with the KGB defector Vladimir Kuzichkin, that the KGB did have some serious reservations about the whole affair.[4] But it was precisely the job of the KGB to present a complete picture of all contingencies, including possible difficulties and complications, especially in the post-invasion task of running the country. And it could only have been expected that these complications would be formidable, if the job was to be done properly. However, it is difficult to imagine that Andropov voted against the final decision, or even abstained – normal Soviet administrative practice would have required him to resign from the KGB chairmanship if either had been the case.

The Soviet Union has a long history of friendly relations with the rulers of Afghanistan, including the Afghan monarchy. A largely feudal, multinational and multiracial country, Afghanistan was clearly not ready for a socialist revolution: what was needed was gradual modernization through economic development. The political situation deteriorated in 1973 and Mohammed Daoud overthrew the monarchy. Daoud himself was overthrown in the 'April Revolution' in 1978, led by pro-Soviet army officers who had been trained in the Soviet Union.[5] The new government declared itself to be Marxist, but when it attempted to transform Afghanistan into a socialist country, a civil war began. This is not an uncommon phenomenon in situations where socialism is imposed upon a feudal, underdeveloped society. Not surprisingly, the Soviet Union, which had been

Afghanistan's main economic partner for decades, supported the new socialist government. However, it became increasingly unstable, and when the President, Mohammed Taraki, who enjoyed Brezhnev's support, was assassinated Soviet intervention could have been forecast. In fact, the army had been demanding an invasion for some time. It finally took place on 29 December 1979.

Was the invasion a miscalculation? It is impossible to answer that question without more information about the actual objectives and their timescale. If Soviet intelligence reports were serious and objective, the present situation must have been predicted. This means that the Soviet government under Brezhnev was prepared to pay the political, military and economic cost of the invasion. At the end of 1979 the political price was actually not very high. Relations with the USA had already seriously deteriorated because the US Senate had made it clear as early as September 1979 that the SALT II treaty would not be ratified. President Carter had searched desperately for a pretext to shelve the treaty, and in the end had resorted to the clumsy device of a Soviet 'combat brigade' in Cuba and demanded its removal – the brigade had actually been there since the 'Cuban Crisis' of 1962. The Soviet government simply ignored this demand. Relations with China were at their lowest level for years – the Chinese invasion of Vietnam at the beginning of 1979 had made a military confrontation with China a real possibility. The revolution in Iran was not welcomed in the Soviet Union; it was a fanatical religious upsurge which interrupted the previously quite good relations between the Soviet Union and the Iranian monarchy. Khomeini's revolution was not only anti-American, it was anti-Soviet as well. Therefore the possibility that the long, 2,000-mile border with Afghanistan could become an additional source of military trouble was probably unthinkable to Soviet military strategists. This border is especially sensitive because on either side of it live Tadzhik, Turkmen and Uzbek peoples and other smaller ethnic groups. The Afghans and Pathans live in the east and south of the country and do not actually constitute a majority. There are also large groups of Hazarars of Mongolian origin and some Iranian groups. The borders between Afghanistan and Pakistan were also artificially created, rather than along ethnic lines. The only true unifying factor of the twenty-odd nations which make up Afghanistan is religion – most of the population are Sunni Moslems.

Soviet military experts might have saved themselves a great deal of trouble if they had read the works of Professor Nikolai Vavilov, a remarkable Soviet scientist and a genuine hero in the struggle for the establishment of scientific principles in Soviet genetics. Vavilov was famous for his botanical–geographical expeditions, of which the most important was to Afghanistan in 1924–26. He visited many parts of the country which had never been seen by Europeans and was the first geographer to make maps of several areas. He also wrote about his expedition, and his description makes it clear that there was a great deal of local hostility, directed both towards him and towards other villages and tribes. Vavilov made a further observation which is probably relevant to current problems in Afghanistan: there was a tradition of culti-vating a unique, fast-growing poppy, *Papaver somniferum*, from which opium is produced and exported.[6] It is now known that the production of opium in Afghanistan increased during the 1960s and 1970s – the remote villages in the main valleys, completely independent from the central govern-ment, were very suitable for cultivation of this crop, which also spread into North Pakistan, where government control was again, non-existent. The Soviet invasion was not only an affront to national pride, it also disrupted the normal opium and heroin trade route. Socialism did not suit the opium traders, and as the war intensified, the main centres of poppy cultivation as well as the opium and heroin trade were transferred to the northern parts of Pakistan, which is now probably the largest centre of heroin production in the world.

The Soviet invasion actually led to an increase in the production of opium and the manufacture of heroin in North
Pakistan and probably in some border areas of Afghanistan
as well. There are several reasons for this. Firstly, most of the
villagers in the border area are now well armed and therefore are not afraid of interference. Secondly, the war has
created a serious refugee problem but at the same time
(particularly since money is needed for food and arms) a
cheap source of labour for the heroin producers. Thirdly,
the energetic measures against the cultivation of *Papaver
somniferum* in Turkey and in Iran under the new Islamic
government drastically curtailed the role of these countries as
drug producers. Heroin from the Herat region of Afghanistan
would normally have crossed through Iran. Now drug
smugglers prefer a route through Pakistan. The measures
against the opium gangs in countries like Thailand have also
been effective, while the border regions of Pakistan are
beyond government control and are much better armed
against any possible punitive action. Heroin and opium
produced in Afghanistan began to penetrate Soviet Central
Asia in 1970, and drug addiction began to become a problem
(though never as serious a problem as in the West). Now all
the drug traffic in this direction has been stopped and the
only open route is to the West. The British media have
reported an increase of 230 per cent in the amount of heroin
seized by customs officers over the last two years, and over
80 per cent of this came from Pakistan.[7]

I have deliberately paid attention to this seemingly insignificant part of the Afghan affair, because this was probably the
main miscalculation of Soviet intelligence – it was dangerous
for the Soviet army to enter well-established centres of drug
production and traffic. The war may continue for years in
such places. It is also true, however, that the drug traffic
aggravates divisions and quarrels between different guerrilla
groups.

Afghanistan is often referred to as the 'Soviet Vietnam'. In
fact, in a military sense the Afghan war is very different from

the war fought by the United States in South-East Asia. The
only thing that they have in common is that both military
campaigns started as an attempt to prevent Chinese domination in the region. The Soviet Union does not need 'victory', nor does it need an unequivocally Communist regime
in Afghanistan. It needs a friendly regime, and one which
has authority over the entire country. It is unrealistic to
imagine that the Soviet Union could simply withdraw from
Afghanistan now, leaving the Karmal government to fight
against numerous hostile military groups and probably lose.
Like the American wish to 'Vietnamize' the war in Vietnam,
the Soviet Union would certainly like to 'Afghanize' the civil
war in Afghanistan. Andropov's main problem (and it was
Brezhnev's main problem as well) is not the absence of a
desire for a negotiated solution, but simply the absence of a
single opposite number with whom to negotiate. In Vietnam
the United States did have a real negotiating partner in the
North Vietnamese government, but the Afghan guerrillas
are not united and their national and tribal differences make
the likelihood of unification improbable. Nor is there any
country which could negotiate on their behalf. Pakistan
could perhaps represent the guerrilla groups, if only because
it is one of the main victims of a war which has brought to it
more than two million Afghan refugees. There is also a
national affinity with some of the Afghan ethnic groups. But
resistance groups in other parts of Afghanistan, represent-
ing other tribes, are unlikely to accept the mediation of
Pakistan.

What can one expect from Andropov in such circumstances? I believe he is likely to propose negotiation to
General Zia of Pakistan, who will probably refuse the offer.
Zia knows that his government cannot control the Pathans
and Afghans, and would have far less influence over the
other nations living in Afghanistan. Like the Iranians, he
will make a preliminary Soviet withdrawal a precondition
for negotiation, which would be absolutely unacceptable to
the Soviet side at present. The Pakistani refusal to enter

negotiations will reduce the political cost of the Soviet presence. The military cost is not very high. There are no signs of discontent about the war in the Soviet military establishment, and there is no anti-war movement in the country at large. 'Afghanization' of the war will apparently be attempted, but it will be a slow, gradual process. The expectation of some Western observers that Andropov will 'move to cut losses in Afghanistan while it is still Brezhnev's war, not his own', and that he may be ready to sacrifice Brezhnev's puppet leader, Babrak Karmal, in order to 'mend fences in the Islamic world, especially with the tempting target of Iran',[8] is wishful thinking. Andropov simply cannot (and probably has no desire to) do this. He will opt for time, and capitalize in propaganda terms on the refusal of Pakistan to talk on behalf of the Afghan resistance. In many respects this war resembles the long war in the Caucasus in the first half of the nineteenth century, as well as the war in Tadzhik, Uzbek and Turkmen areas in the second half of the nineteenth century and the civil war in Soviet Central Asia in 1919–28. The Sovietization of the Moslem areas of the Soviet Union was a very long process, and continued until the early 1930s.

Babrak Karmal was warmly welcomed in Moscow at the end of December 1982 and given the honour of speaking at the Supreme Soviet jubilee session. If Vladimir Kuzichkin is correct in thinking that Karmal has collaborated with the KGB for many years, and if he is also right when he says that Andropov advised support for Karmal rather than Taraki as long ago as 1978,[9] there is every chance that he will retain that support now, when Andropov is no longer an adviser to Brezhnev but the Party General Secretary.

Soviet policy towards the Middle East and Eastern Europe

The two areas in which there has been little change in Soviet policy are the Middle East and Eastern Europe. Soviet involvement in the Middle East, started initially by Khrushchev, has always been extremely expensive and there have been very few positive rewards. The enormous political and economic investments made in Egypt have been lost, and the Soviet Union is left with only two truly friendly countries, Syria and South Yemen. Sudan, Somalia, Iraq and Algeria are either unfriendly or keep their distance, while Libya is more of an embarrassment than an asset. This situation is partly due to a historic change in Soviet policy, a change which was probably an error. Stalin concentrated his attention on neighbouring rather than distant countries and preferred to support parties rather than individuals. It is unthinkable that he would have treated Nasser or the leaders of the Ba'ath Party in Iraq and Syria as friends, giving them generous aid while ignoring the fact that Communist parties in their countries were illegal and that Communists had been imprisoned or executed. Of course, the Soviet Union did not then have the resources for a global policy, and it can be argued that this made concentration on the task of maintaining a safe and friendly immediate environment inevitable. It was natural that Khrushchev should seek to broaden Soviet foreign interests, but his tendency to place trust in individual leaders, regardless of the nature of the political and social institutions in their countries was disastrous. He cultivated friendly relations with men like Nasser, who were pro-Soviet but also anti-Communist. Explaining why Soviet intellectuals did not support Soviet Middle East policy in 1967, Roy Medvedev wrote anonymously in his *Political Diary*:

> It is no secret to [the Soviet intelligentsia] nor to [Soviet workers] that not millions, but billions of roubles are required to arm the UAR and to build the Aswan dam there, thousands of kilometres from the USSR, as well as dozens of other enterprises. Our aid to Egypt – military, financial and economic – exceeds our aid to any socialist country, and possibly to all the socialist countries together. Given our

many unresolved domestic problems, this quantity of aid to Egypt can hardly be considered sensible. Objections to this huge expenditure on Egypt are the stronger because very few members of the intelligentsia consider Nasser and his friends to be socialists. The view that he is a fascist or a national socialist is widespread. In any case, it is well known that there is no real democracy in Egypt. Communists are harshly repressed. In the time that we have been friendly with Egypt there have been a number of bloody anti-communist campaigns. Communists have been imprisoned, tortured and killed. In the short period that Egypt and Syria were united, there were serious repressions of the communists in Syria too.[10]

This heavy political and economic investment, on no better grounds than friendly relations between leaders, meant that the Soviet Union paid a very heavy price when President Sadat decided to change Egypt's political orientation after Nasser's death, having first extracted all he could from the Soviet Union to prepare for the Yom Kippur war in 1973. This is only one example of a policy which, with a few amendments, was continued by Brezhnev, and for which Brezhnev paid a similar political price in Somalia and Zimbabwe.

The first signs of change began to appear in 1980, after the outbreak of the Iraq–Iran war. In spite of heavy commitments in Iraq and a treaty of friendship and co-operation, the Soviet Union decided to follow a safe, neutral course. After the loss of billions in Egypt and of military installations in Somalia, the Soviet Union also changed its arms sales policy in the region. Arms are now supplied only for cash, not on the basis of long-term credits and loans.

The new leadership will probably be much less generous in giving economic and military assistance to pro-Soviet but unstable and dictatorial regimes (like Ethiopia) without insisting on structural changes in the form of a Soviet-style one-party system. The most likely policy is for the Soviet Union to have fewer 'close friends' but more reliable partners with stable social systems that are less vulnerable to coups. Soviet involvement in Syria is too deep to be withdrawn, but Iraq will be dropped and will probably cease to be a recipient of Soviet aid. There were speculations in Israel that Andropov might adopt a more balanced, less pro-Arab policy. Perhaps the most Israel should expect from Andropov are measures to reduce anti-Semitism within the Soviet Union. This could, in turn, reduce the Soviet Jewish community's pressure to emigrate. There may be some Soviet moves towards the more conservative Arab nations, primarily Saudi Arabia, for purely economic reasons. The Soviet Union plans to increase its sales of oil and gas for hard currency, and therefore does not want a serious drop in international oil prices. Achieving this will require some co-ordination of oil trade policy with the other major oil producers.

There are no signs yet of a change in the basic principles of Soviet policy towards Eastern Europe. In 1957–67 Andropov was the main architect of this policy, and the fact that his chief assistants in the Central Committee Department which deals with socialist countries have remained there under their new boss K. G. Rusakov probably indicates that this policy continues. Andropov will certainly support the trend towards economic integration, but he will also try to learn from the Eastern European experience and not force East European countries to accept the Soviet model in all its details. In his speech at the Plenum of the Central Committee on 22 November 1982, he remarked that the Soviet Union should make better use of the experience of friendly socialist countries. This was perceived as a possible hint that some elements of the Hungarian model of socialism would be introduced in the Soviet Union. But this conclusion is premature. It would be beneficial if the current restrictions on travel to and from socialist countries were lifted, and, in particular, if tourist and business travel between the Soviet Union and its Eastern European allies was made easier. Andropov seemed to be satisfied with recent developments in Poland and the Polish situation is probably no longer perceived as an emergency by the Soviet leadership.

Events in Western Europe will have a major influence on Soviet policy in Eastern Europe. If the USA succeeds in stationing Pershing II and Cruise missiles in Germany and other countries, the introduction of Soviet-made Cruise missiles into East Germany and Czechoslovakia will be inevitable. This will be a complicated task, because these countries have no Soviet missiles at present and installing them could provoke a genuine anti-nuclear movement.

The Eastern European regimes are varied, and Andropov understands this much better than Brezhnev did. As former Ambassador to Hungary, as Head of the Foreign Department on socialist countries, and as head of the KGB, he has had to deal with the nations of Eastern Europe on a level which gives him a good insight into their specific situations. Before Brezhnev became General Secretary, he had no experience in foreign affairs, and later he was occupied, for the most part, with business relations with other heads of state. However, practically all Eastern European countries face difficult economic problems because of their extensive borrowing from the West. The substantial repayments will not permit them to improve living standards for several years: a situation which does not favour the liberalization of political life. Economic integration with the Soviet Union would only increase their 'satellite' character. Before 1980 there were centrifugal forces inside the Soviet bloc. Now the pressure is centripetal, and this tendency is likely to continue. I do not think that Andropov will be too generous in giving Soviet allies economic aid, since they cannot afford political independence now anyway. Even Romania is likely to be less maverick in her diplomatic activity, and will toe the line better than before.

The United States and Western Europe

The change of leadership in Moscow was a much more rapid, smooth and orderly process than either the American or the European governments had expected. The *Wall Street Journal* reported Brezhnev's death on 12 November 1982 under the headline 'A Fight for Succession is Likely to Complicate Many Soviet Problems'. However, by the time this paper appeared, it was late afternoon in Moscow and the succession process was practically over. The prediction that the short-term leadership would be 'reluctant or even unable to adopt any policy changes' was proved wrong the following day, when the proceedings of the Central Committee meeting of 12 November became known, and there were clear signs of changes in foreign policy three days later at the Kremlin reception for foreign leaders after the funeral.

The American government was prepared for Brezhnev's death, but it was absolutely unprepared for any serious change in Soviet foreign policy and it had not worked out any possible responses to various alternatives. All the issues which emerged from the rapid new Soviet moves were dealt with in the USA on an *ad hoc* basis or simply dismissed as propaganda. Only a few weeks later the Reagan administration realized that it should be engaged in serious dialogue and discussions, but by then it had already lost the initiative. Andropov, who had been in power for a mere two weeks, seemed to be winning the diplomatic battle against his opposite number in the USA, who was already at 'mid-term', having completed two years in office.

Andropov had one great advantage over Reagan even at the very start of his tenure in office. He knew much more about the United States than Reagan knew about the Soviet Union. He had more competent advisers on American affairs than the Reagan administration had on the Soviet Union. Professor Georgii Arbatov, Director of the Institute of the United States and Canada, is a close friend of

Andropov's, and the academics in his institute are, for the most part, extremely competent in their fields. Andropov's son Igor, now a diplomat, was a senior researcher there for several years. The only member of the White House staff to specialize in the Soviet Union, Professor Richard Pipes, was better known as a historian of Czarist Russia (and for his anti-Soviet views and lack of tact.) He has now returned to Harvard. Reagan, however, was not short of unsolicited advice: the change of leadership in Moscow gave past Presidents and past policy makers the public opportunity to express their views to his administration, and to European leaders as well. Richard Nixon, Jimmy Carter, Henry Kissinger, Zbigniew Brzezinski and many others gave interviews and wrote articles on the general problem of 'How to deal with Moscow'. Very few of their recommendations were relevant to the new situation, and no-one predicted accurately the way in which Soviet policy towards the USA and Western Europe would change.

Nixon, who wanted Reagan to attend Brezhnev's funeral, was the most realistic in his assessment of America's ability to influence Soviet policy. He advised a delaying response to Andropov's disarmament offers, with a West European–Japanese–American meeting preceding a Soviet–American summit. However, Nixon's view of the influence of personality, or of the media, on Soviet decision-making appears a little unrealistic:

> Among other things, Nixon says, 'I want 270 million Soviets to see President Reagan on TV – to see he is not a monster, but a very decent, attractive leader.'[11]

No-one in the Soviet Union is likely to be really impressed by Reagan's television image. Nobody thinks he is a 'monster' – he is perceived, more or less accurately, as a right-wing conservative anti-Communist. Television does not make policy in the Soviet Union. If 'socialism with a human face' is an abstraction, 'monetarism with a human face' is irrelevant: broad smiles on television will have no effect on reality.

Henry Kissinger suggested that since the Soviet side would be extremely slow and reluctant to take any new initiatives, the United States now had an opportunity of gaining an advantage.

> If, however, we pre-empt the negotiating process with a bold program, we have a chance to dominate both diplomacy and public discussion. . . We should seize every opportunity to put before them negotiating proposals that reflect *our* definitions of genuine arms control, proper economic relations and restrained international conduct. It can only be to our advantage to negotiate from our agenda, not theirs.[12]

This was good advice, but it did not work out that way: America was pre-empted and left to negotiate from 'Andropov's agenda'. Brzezinski's advice was essentially the same. Americans 'are in a position to move him [Andropov] in one direction or to push him into another . . . we will be defining the agenda for the debate instead of having them debate how they can best do us in.[13]

In fact, the American delegation which talked to Andropov on 15 November 1982 probably did not report any signs of an improvement in Soviet attitudes. Apparently Andropov, like his predecessor, held the United States responsible for the deterioration in relations, and he was unlikely to be the first to make conciliatory gestures.

It was clear from the first days of Andropov's leadership that the essence of his new policy would be not an attempt to please the Americans, *but to compete with the United States for the hearts and minds of the West European nations*, both their people and their governments. The main part of this new policy would, of course, be the problem of nuclear and conventional arms. 1983 is a crucial year for possible success or irreparable failure, and I was absolutely sure that Andropov would lose no time in offering new ideas. However, even my prediction of rapid and energetic attempts to reduce the military tension in Europe[14] underestimated the policy which quickly came to be called 'Andropov's peace offensive'. It was a clever and unexpected move and I shall discuss it separately in the following section.

Under both the Carter and the Reagan administrations American policy towards the Soviet Union was inconsistent and unpredictable. The decline of détente actually started after Nixon's resignation, when Senator Henry Jackson got support for the 'Jackson Amendment' to the trade bill which made the lifting of restrictions on trade with the USSR dependent upon a specific number of Soviet Jews being allowed to emigrate. (The effect was to reduce emigration immediately.) When Carter began his presidency with a letter to Andrei Sakharov, the most famous Soviet dissident, in January 1977, before he had written to any Soviet official, and when he made new offers for disarmament in the middle of the SALT II process, he showed complete ignorance about the way the Soviet political system works. Later the introduction of his ill-conceived 'Grain embargo', Reagan's 'Siberian gas pipeline embargo', and the cancellation of many commercial contracts by US firms along with US embargoes against European firms which tried to honour their agreements, were all seen as unilateral moves (although linked with events in Afghanistan and Poland) in the American 'trade war' against the Soviet Union. By November 1982 many of these measures had already been lifted (without any Soviet pressure), since they were damaging the economy of the United States, as well as relations with Europe. Americans had exaggerated the effectiveness both of the economic pressure they could bring to bear and of Soviet dependence on Western technology, but their political rhetoric remained essentially unchanged.

Nonetheless, the need for a Soviet–American summit had been under discussion for some time while Brezhnev was still alive, and President Reagan seemed to regard the idea positively. A Reagan performance against Brezhnev would, of course, have been rather impressive. For that very reason a possible summit between Brezhnev and Reagan in 1982 was not desired by the Soviet side, simply because of fears

that Brezhnev would perform poorly. He would certainly
not have been able to take part in a flexible exchange of
views, but only to read prepared statements. The idea of a
summit had been discussed, however, and the subsequent
change in Moscow made it desirable to hold it as soon as
possible, the more so because of the crucial problems in
East–West relations that had to be settled in 1983. Once the
US embarked on its MX missile programme and installed
Cruise and Pershing missiles in Europe, discussion of these
and other issues would be much more difficult. However,
Reagan was silent, probably hoping for a positive MX
decision in Congress. This gave Andropov the initiative. He
would most likely have preferred to respond to a Reagan
offer, which is why he did not mention a summit conference
in his speech to the Central Committee, or during his speech
at the session of the Supreme Soviet on 21 December 1982.
However, at the end of December, he answered questions
which had been submitted 'through the Soviet Embassy in
Washington by Joseph Kingsbury-Smith, national editor of
the Hearst newspapers'. His answers, which were distributed by TASS and published in Soviet papers on New
Year's Eve, included a message of good will to the American
people. He outlined a programme for disarmament in 1983,
suggested a nuclear freeze and a 25 per cent reduction in all
nuclear arsenals, and replied positively to 'former President
Nixon's appeal' for a summit with Reagan. Andropov stres-
sed the point that meetings at the summit level are always
welcome but should, of course, be well prepared in advance.

The first reaction from Washington was negative. Alan
Romberg, the US State Department deputy spokesman,
said: that 'he knew of "no active intention or plan to arrange
a summit"'. He said the administration stands by a statement
last month by George P. Schultz that a summit would be
premature.'[15] It was clear that Reagan was not ready for a
summit meeting, perhaps did not want one at all. With the
departure of Professor Pipes, the White House and State
Department were left without an adviser who had a reason-

able knowledge of the Soviet Union. The President appeared to be on the defensive, explaining that he was in favour of a summit in principle, but that it should be very carefully prepared with guarantees of positive results. This unenthusiastic response may have been due to a fear that exposure on television, while proving that Reagan is not a 'monster', might, nevertheless, have shown him to lack competence when faced with complex problems of nuclear disarmament and international affairs, and to rely much more on his advisers than the more professional Andropov.

At the end of December 1982 the Central Intelligence Agency unexpectedly declassified their 401-page report about the Soviet economy which had been made available to Congress at the end of November.[16] The new CIA report completely contradicted opinions expressed in the US media about the Soviet economy, to the effect that it is on the verge of collapse. It also contradicted many of President Reagan's earlier statements about the Soviet Union, which had been made to justify the economic blockade introduced in response to events in Poland. In spite of some problems and disproportions in the Soviet economy, the report testified that it is, in general 'in good shape' and developing more rapidly than its American counterpart. It is also essentially self-sufficient, and 'the ability of the Soviet economy to remain viable in the absence of imports is much greater than that of most, possibly all, other industrialised economies.'[17]

Soviet–American détente as negotiated by Brezhnev included mutual trade as a basic element of the package. However, America proved to be an unreliable trading partner, linking trade with political demands and clearly overestimating Soviet dependence upon American technology. Commercial circles in the United States realized later that this policy had a more harmful effect at home than in the Soviet Union: in trade it is the producer left with unsold manufactured goods who suffers more than the purchaser left with unspent currency. There have been no indications in Andropov's speeches, or in other high-level comments in

the Soviet press, that the new leadership wants to revive
Soviet–American trade or to continue making large purchases of American grain. The Soviet Union has completely
ignored Reagan's offer to the USSR in 1982–83, made
before Brezhnev's death, to sell an extra 17 million metric
tonnes of grain. A one-year extension of the grain purchase
agreement, according to which the Soviet Union will buy
about 6 million tonnes annually from the United States, was
made in September. But a Soviet offer to make a new agreement, or extend the current one, is very unlikely. The attitude towards trade with the EEC will be similar. The Soviet
Union refused, in December, to buy surplus European butter
offered at a smaller discount than usual as a 'punishment'
for events in Afghanistan and Poland. The EEC simply lost
out on the deal.

It is absolutely obvious that the new leadership will enter
into no trading agreements that come with strings attached.
Both Khrushchev and Brezhnev made many promises about
food production, and tied their personal prestige to agricultural reforms which they expected to create an abundance
of food. When these reforms did not work, large purchases
of foreign food were necessary to cover up the failures and
protect the reputations of the leaders. Andropov has not tied
his prestige to such promises. Apparently he prefers to make
collective farms work harder and more efficiently, rather
than covering up their shortcomings by purchases abroad.
Food purchases will, of course be necessary. But trade will
only take place with countries which are considered to be
'reliable' partners. It will be used to increase Soviet influence, not Soviet vulnerability. Up to now the Western
countries, even those which have wanted to increase trade
with the Soviet Union, have tried to use trade for propaganda
purposes – to gain maximum publicity for the idea that the
socialist system cannot work without Western technology.
This notion was essentially false. Trade with the West constitutes only about 5 per cent of Soviet economic turnover,
and more than half of this foreign trade is with close neigh-

bours like Finland, Austria, Japan or Sweden. The situation was different in Poland or Hungary, and this is why the recession in the West hit them so badly. I predict that trade with the Soviet Union for the propaganda purposes will not be so easy in future, and that only friendly trading partners can expect substantial Soviet orders. Already in December the leading journal of Soviet trade, *Ekonomicheskaya gazeta* (*The Economic Gazette*), had significantly increased the number of its advertisements for Japanese industrial products, and was not publishing any advertisements for West European equipment. Japan has for years been an extremely reliable trading partner, never mixing trade with ideology.

The slow and inadequate American reaction to several important Soviet proposals (usually dismissed as 'pure propaganda') has become an important source of European dissatisfaction. At first European leaders too were rather dismissive, and tried to ignore the Soviet initiatives. However, the attitude of the general public in Western Europe towards the Soviet Union is different from that in the USA. For the countries of Western Europe the Soviet Union is a neighbour, a country which for centuries has been an integral part of the traditional balance of power. Europeans know that the Soviet preoccupation with defence has a valid justification, since Russia has been invaded twice from the West, and once from Japan, in the twentieth century alone. Andropov's peace initiatives and ideas about legitimate European security needs can, of course, be treated as propaganda. But it is very efficient propaganda and it has begun to shift public opinion away from conservative policies in such crucial countries as West Germany, Britain, Italy and Holland. The only test to distinguish propaganda from realistic and serious proposals is negotiation, and the reluctance of the American administration to begin negotiations has dismayed some leaders of Western Europe. This is clear in the case of Germany, and is also true of Britain; in both countries pre-election debates have focused attention on these issues. In the final analysis it is Western Europe which is the real hostage of Soviet–American rivalry, and it is difficult to ignore the Soviet initiative for too long. When the Warsaw Pact summit convened in Prague at the beginning of 1983 and adopted a long and comprehensive 'Political Declaration'[18] it finally became impossible to shelve the issue any longer. European leaders began to make positive comments and statements. Western Europe slowly started to move towards some accommodation with the new Soviet leadership, leaving America behind. Reagan lost his leading role: he was trailing events and on the defensive, frustrated, under criticism from his allies, uncertain about a proper response, raising irrelevant objections.

Within two months the new leadership in the Soviet Union was able to take the initiative in the diplomatic and propaganda battle for Western Europe. Reagan's policy was based on the assumption that the United States would be able to exploit a long and destructive power struggle in the Kremlin to its advantage, and he had no alternative strategy. This has shown quite clearly that diplomacy and politics remain an art, in which it is not difficult to distinguish professionals from amateurs. The situation in the middle of January 1983 was well reflected in the cover cartoon of London's *The Economist* (15–21 January) – a large and powerful dove with Andropov's face is pressing his foot on a small and confused eagle with the face of Reagan. Vice-President Bush's 'shuttle' trip through several West European capitals at the end of January and beginning of February did nothing to change the situation, for Bush offered no genuinely new ideas or constructive proposals.

Andropov's peace offensive

By the end of November many Western magazines and newspapers were already writing about Andropov's 'peace offensive'. However, it really began in earnest with his speech at the jubilee session of the Supreme Soviet on 21 December 1982, and continued in unabated flow during the following weeks. By the middle of January 1983 the West had about twenty new proposals, in various military fields, to consider. Some were perhaps not really new, but in 1983 their impact was different than it would have been ten or twenty years previously, when Western superiority in nuclear arms meant that the Soviet Union was speaking from a position of comparative weakness. Moreover, the West did not have so large and powerful a disarmament movement ten or twenty years ago. By 1982–3 this movement had become a serious political factor in every democratic country.

The main stimulus for the many new proposals was, of course, the problem of the 572 Cruise and Pershing II missiles which are due to become operational in Western Europe at the end of 1983. The position of both sides was clear from the end of 1981. The Soviet Union was prepared to reduce the number of its medium-range nuclear missiles in the European parts of the Soviet Union (both the older SS4s and SS5s with a single warhead each, and the new, more accurate SS-20s, each with three independently targeted warheads), in return for cancellation of the plan to site a new generation of American missiles in Europe. President Reagan responded with his 'zero option', an undertaking to cancel the installation of the new missiles if the USSR would destroy its entire arsenal of medium-range missiles, including those which are located behind the Ural mountains, which could, theoretically, strike Norway, if re-targeted from their present Eastern destinations. The 'zero option' was immediately rejected as unrealistic since NATO would still be left with the British and French intermediate-range and strategic missiles which are targeted against the Soviet Union. Confidential bilateral talks have begun in Geneva to resolve this impasse. If the talks are unsuccessful, the American plans will go ahead. By November 1982 there was no indication that any progress had been made.

In his speech on 21 December 1982[19] Andropov introduced a new proposal which seemed a reasonable and more
realistic version of the 'zero option'. His idea was quite
simple. The Soviet Union would keep in Europe 'only as
many missiles as are kept by France and Britain and not one
more'. This could mean a reduction by two-thirds – from as
many as 600 missiles to about 150. In subsequent discussions
it was hinted that the extra missiles would be destroyed and
not just shifted to the East. This offer was almost immediately
rejected by France, Britain and the USA, largely on the
grounds that the new US missiles were for the protection of
West Germany and other NATO countries that do not have
their own nuclear forces. This argument seemed illogical –
Britain is an active member of NATO, and France, although
not part of the joint military structure, is still under an
obligation to use its military forces to protect Germany.
British and French troops are stationed in Germany and
West Berlin. To consider the British and French nuclear
forces as purely national nuclear deterrents contradicts
the meaning and purpose of the North Atlantic alliance.
Andropov's offer made it clear that Britain's plan to change
from Polaris missiles to Trident, which would substantially
increase both the number of British missiles and the number
of warheads, would be matched by an increase in the number
of Soviet missiles targeted against Britain and Western
Europe. Reagan's 'zero option' was probably intended to be
unacceptable, in order that the plans for the deployment of
Pershing and Cruise missiles could go ahead. Andropov's
insistence that British and French missiles be included in the
balance destroyed the viability of 'zero option' completely.
Andropov also decided that the secrecy of the Geneva talks
was not in Soviet interests, since their position in the negotiations was more reasonable than the American one. In these
circumstances secrecy only favoured the United States.
Many Western politicians and commentators have argued
that the new Soviet proposals are designed for propaganda
purposes, and that additional pressure may force the Soviet

Union to agree to the 'zero option', or to something similar. But this interpretation suggests a misjudgement of Soviet priorities: an equality of missiles with Western Europe is most probably the bottom line below which they will not be persuaded to go. They would certainly never agree to the destruction of all their medium-range missiles. An immediate objection to Andropov's December proposals arose on the question of differences in missile capability. Soviet SS-20s have three warheads, while French missiles have only one. British Polaris missiles also have three warheads, but they are not independently targeted. However, the Trident system, which the British government has opted for, is more formidable: each missile has ten independently targeted nuclear warheads. Despite predictions to the contrary the Soviet side accepted the possibility of an agreement based upon parity in the number of warheads, rather than missiles.

A few days later, in the interview with Kingsbury-Smith mentioned earlier, Andropov suggested a reduction by 25 per cent of all intercontinental missiles in the Soviet Union and in the United States. This offer was again dismissed as propaganda or ignored by the West.

Peace proposals took up a major part of the agenda at the Warsaw Pact meeting in Prague on 3–5 January. The 'Political Declaration' issued by this meeting was a serious document on nuclear disarmament, aiming at more than straightforward nuclear reduction and control. It also included a reduction in conventional armed forces, a reduction in the arms trade, the prohibition of all nuclear tests, and the elimination of radiological weapons and the neutron bomb. The declaration also suggested that

> Nato and the Warsaw pact should sign a treaty renouncing the use of force against each other; this could later be extended to other countries. Agreements on arms control should be properly verified, where necessary by 'international procedures'.[20]

A reduction in naval forces, the limitation of military spending and a freeze on the development and introduction of the new nuclear weapon systems were also recommended. There were proposals for 'nuclear free zones' – for example, the exclusion from the Mediterranean of all ships carrying nuclear weapons. And in response to recent discussions deploring the very high cost of the superpower arms race to developing countries as well, a waste of funds that could be used for rather more humane purposes, the declaration proposed that the financial and material savings which would be made as a result of the reduction in military programmes should be used for social and economic development and for economic assistance to the Third World.

This document was also initially dismissed as propaganda. The immediate reaction of some Western leaders and of the conservative press was that the Soviet aim was more a question of splitting the West than of making peace. Two or three days later the tone of comments changed: Western leaders began to say that they would study the offer seriously. Perhaps the most relevant reaction came from West Germany, where the outcome of the elections on 6 March 1983 could be affected if the politicians dismiss the opportunity for a reduction in the arms race. Helmut Kohl's victory in Germany was not directly related to the missile problem. However, the entry of the anti-nuclear Greens into the Bundestag was a direct result of the missile issue. The Greens will probably have an impact on future policy. The most crucial components of the new American missile package – the Pershing II missiles which will be able to reach Moscow in six minutes and are designed to destroy Soviet command structures – are to be deployed in Germany, the shortest distance from their potential targets.

By 7 January Francis Pym, the British Foreign Secretary, stated that the Prague declaration

> was 'a document of great significance' . . . he indicated an important degree of flexibility in European thought, which meant that the British Government was certainly ready to consider what he called 'second best' in reducing missiles on both sides of the East–West divide.[21]

An editorial in the *Sunday Telegraph* suggested that

> it is not enough for Western leaders to be curtly dismissive
> about Mr Andropov's calculated overtures. The man-in-
> the-street hears plausible-sounding talk of peace from the
> new ruler of a super-power; he listens for at least an echo
> from his own leaders.[22]

Finally President Reagan himself realized that his negative
and dismissive response might cost him his project of installing the new generation of American missiles in Europe at
the end of the year. These missiles were crucial to United
States strategy – they are to be under 100 per cent American
control and would reduce the time in which American
nuclear weapons could reach Soviet targets from thirty to
five or six minutes. Reagan was also in the middle of his
difficult task of finding a proper mode of deployment for the
new strategic MX missiles. His 'dense pack' mode had been
rejected on technical grounds, and the whole MX project
was in jeopardy. The Soviet Union was not in fact against
the MX missiles in principle, if they were to replace missiles
already deployed. But the 'dense pack' deployment 'violates
a central provision of the SALT I and SALT II arms agreements – the requirement that neither side create any new
fixed underground launchers'.[23] Although the Reagan administration argued that dense pack skirts this provision by
means of a neat technical trick, many experts did not agree
with this casuistry. Paul Warnke, 'who led the US negotiating effort for SALT II, disagrees vehemently with the
Reagan Administration's interpretation. "Dense Pack is a
violation of both SALT I and SALT II".'[24]

The two main projects on which the Reagan administration based its plans for military and strategic superiority
were thus in danger of being rejected. Moreover, the enormous
budget deficit made some serious cuts in military spending
inevitable. The seriousness of the situation dawned upon the
administration in the middle of January, and at this stage,
Reagan lost the initiative completely. His first decision was

symbolic – to send Vice-President George Bush to Europe ostensibly on a fact-finding and propaganda mission, but with the actual intention of pressing European leaders to carry on with the Cruise and Pershing programme. His second decision was irrational – he abruptly dismissed Eugene Rostow, Head of the Arms Control and Disarmament Agency. This action was immediately criticized in the Western media as bordering on panic. It was badly timed and clumsily executed, and indicated a lack of consistency in American disarmament policy.

The new chief appointed by Reagan, Kenneth Adelman, had no previous experience of arms control or disarmament. Confirmation by the Senate of his appointment was recently postponed for these reasons; the delay may take weeks and the outcome, at the time of writing, is by no means certain. It was clear, therefore, that Reagan wanted to postpone the negotiations, and was manufacturing excuses. Vice-President Bush's European trip did not produce any new developments, except a very general reference in passing to Reagan's readiness to eliminate all medium-range missiles from the surface of the earth. It seemed clear that the American priority was to launch the rearmament programme and restore military superiority. After many months of fruitless discussions on disarmament, there were suddenly new offers from the Soviet Union which were negotiable, attractive to Europeans as a 'second best' deal and accompanied by signs that the Soviet Union might make further concessions short of the 'zero option'. These proposals would be acceptable to all parties, except for Reagan and some ultra-conservatives who do not actually want a real agreement. They are determined to place Pershing II and Cruise missiles in Europe.

Rostow was dismissed without any consultation with Reagan's own Secretary of State or with any Western government. On the same day NATO governments were, on the one hand, seeking explanations from the United States whether this dismissal 'will have any direct effect on the prospects in the Geneva nuclear arms negotiations with the Soviet Union which reopen in two weeks',[25] and, on the other, trying to assess a statement by the German Social Democrat candidate for Chancellor, Mr Hans-Jochen Vogel, who had just returned from Moscow with some extremely promising new ideas for negotiations. Inevitably the European media expressed doubts about whether Reagan actually *wants* real disarmament. The European governments had agreed to accept the new American missiles if the Geneva talks on European arms reductions did not produce results by the end of 1983. It was taken for granted that if this happened, it would be because of Soviet inflexibility – nobody was prepared for a scenario in which the American side was responsible for a stalemate. Before Brezhnev's death, both sides had been inflexible. Now the Soviet side had suddenly started to offer attractive compromise proposals, so that unless the American negotiating team too was prepared to depart from its opening 'zero option' position, the negotiations would be pointless. Rostow had showed signs of being flexible, so he had to go.

For America, Pershing II and Cruise missiles in Europe mean much more than protecting Western Europe from the Soviet army. These missiles are suitable as a first-strike weapon, and would be the first American nuclear weapons on the Continent without dual American–European (host country) control. They also represent a new generation of missiles – the Soviet Union does not yet have anything comparable in accuracy or invulnerability. In a technical sense they represent a qualitatively new stage of the arms race, and could give the USA qualitative superiority. Moreover, it is unrealistic to argue that the MX missiles (which violate SALT I and II) and this new generation of 'European missiles' could contribute to disarmament ('force the Russians to retreat'). They mean a new spiral of the arms race, which would become much more expensive and much more dangerous.

It would be much easier for the Soviet Union to impose

new sacrifices on its people if the arms race began again in earnest than it would for the West. This is not only because of the absence of a democratic peace movement. The simple psychological fact that the new American Pershing and Cruise missiles would threaten the Soviet Union from *German territory* is extremely relevant. The Soviet public is not unduly concerned about the French or British independent nuclear forces – neither of these countries is perceived as a possible aggressor against the Soviet Union. But Germany is a special case, for reasons which need no explanation here. If a West German government (whether conservative or social democratic) thinks that Soviet–German détente, trade and friendly political relations could survive the appearance on German soil of a new generation of American missiles, then it is indulging in wishful thinking. West Germany can have the missiles, but it will mean the end of détente and probably of a number of trade agreements as well. The new missiles would also change the general atmosphere in Germany – to justify them it would be necessary to raise the level of anti-Soviet propaganda and to accept a variety of Cold War supplements to the new weapons systems. Simple logic makes this obvious. This prospect will slowly filter through to the minds of the public in Western Europe, and 'Andropov's peace offensive' will continue to stress it. America will certainly lose the propaganda battle. And even if they succeed in installing their new missiles in Europe, they will make Europe a much more nervous place, with a more powerful peace movement and an inevitable increase in anti-American feeling and 'leftism'. American pressure to include Spain in NATO certainly contributed to the socialist victory in Spain in 1982, while the problem of American nuclear bases had a similar effect in Greece. Nor are the new missiles electoral assets for the British or the German Conservative Parties. In their blind drive towards strategic superiority, the American ultraconservatives may lose much more than their many military bases in Europe.

Conclusion

The question which everyone in the Soviet Union and, to a lesser extent, outside it as well is now asking is: are we really witnessing the beginning of a new era in Soviet history? After Stalin's death in 1953 the answer was a clear and positive 'yes'. In his own way, Stalin was a brutal but successful leader and a skilful politician. Under his rule industry expanded rapidly, the Soviet Union won a devastating war and made a speedy post-war economic recovery. It became a superpower, and a Soviet empire (or 'socialist bloc', as it is called in the USSR) came into existence. If Beria, Malenkov or Molotov (the latter two are still alive) had come to power after Stalin rather than Khrushchev, the main pillars of the Stalinist system and his methods of repression and coercion would probably have continued for some time; monuments to him would still be standing all over the country. Repressive and tyrannical though the system was, it was nonetheless viable and efficient in its own way. With China as a new member, the Communist camp was extremely powerful, and was expanding in the eastern part of the world. People under Communist regimes were very poor and without civil rights, but the power of the state was enormous. Under Malenkov or Molotov the government and Party systems would probably have been less brutal, but in a historical sense the Stalin era would have continued. Fortunately for the Soviet Union, things turned out differently. But the 'Khrushchev phenomenon' was by no means inevitable.

Khrushchev changed the Stalinist system in a number of ways, if not entirely. For that reason it makes historical sense to talk about a 'Khrushchev era' in Soviet history. Things were hardly perfect, but there was an improvement, and the world as a whole was a safer place. Under Khrushchev there was a partial restoration of legality, the elimination of brutal terror, and rehabilitation of millions of victims. He may have made numerous errors in his handling of the economy and of agriculture, but in political terms he transformed the Soviet Union into a more liberal, more open society. The eleven years of Khrushchev's rule certainly constitute a distinct period, so much so that some authors, like Solzhenitsyn, argue that it was an aberration. The power of the Soviet state was no longer growing so quickly, the Soviet empire suffered a severe blow as a result of the conflict with China, but the main groups within the country, workers, peasants and intellectuals, gained much more influence in the running of society. In 1964 there were certainly good reasons for Khrushchev's retirement. It is most likely that he would have been replaced in a democratic society as well, but in that case the positive features of his regime would have been preserved. However, the abrupt end of Khrushchev's rule in 1964 was essentially a change towards conservativism. It was not a question of the personal victory of Brezhnev or of Suslov but rather a victory for the bureaucratic Party and state apparatus which hated Khrushchev for his periodic administrative reorganizations.

Brezhnev was not a real leader in 1964, but the representative of the bureaucracy which sought a quieter, safer, more secure, privileged life. His constituency was the bureaucratic elite. In this sense Brezhnev also changed the system, for he, more than anyone else, created the conditions for the growth of a truly privileged ruling elite, a real *nomenklatura*. In political terms the outstanding feature of his rule was the reversal of the liberal process, the limited restoration of repression and the complete halt of all rehabilitations. But Brezhnev brought some element of stability to the Soviet

Union, and the predictability of growth. This trend was welcomed at home and abroad, but only up to a point. Already by 1975–76 this stability was turning into stagnation, and the bureaucratic elite, secure and isolated, was growing old, corrupt and inefficient. Again it was the absence of democratic processes which allowed Brezhnev's power to drag on beyond its natural duration.

Do the changes which are taking place after Brezhnev's death mean the beginning of a new political era in Soviet history? A change of generation is, of course, inevitable, but does that necessarily imply serious political innovation which can shape the political system as a whole? The answer is still unclear. There has been a change of style, an attempt at better management, the signs of a more flexible approach to problems of foreign policy. But there have been no developments significant enough to be viewed as either political or economic reform. Current policy is probably better constructed, better implemented, more skilfully presented, but it is still *the same conservative policy without any sign of liberal or democratic trends*. However, the very fact that it is more flexible, more efficient, and more decisive may stimulate reforms, as soon as experience proves that the demand for better discipline (the slogan of the day), is not enough to bring about lasting improvements. This is, to be sure, an optimistic scenario. So far there is no clear direction, and various alternatives remain open.

The situation is rather similar to previous periods of succession. When Lenin died in 1924 there was no clear path ahead. It would have been possible to continue the New Economic Policy (a mixed capitalist and socialist economy) and to orient the country essentially towards internal development. There was also the more radical alternative of 'permanent revolution', i.e. the attempt to stimulate revolution in other countries so as to provide support for the Bolshevik revolution in Russia. The first alternative was supported by Stalin, Bukharin and the Party apparatus, which wanted stability; the second was favoured by Trotsky and the 'Left opposition'. The more moderate Stalinist faction won, and their alternative was probably the better one for the 1920s. Unfortunately, Stalin himself changed course in 1929; he destroyed NEP, imposed the brutal forced collectivization of agriculture, vastly increased the power of the security organs and finally introduced his own personal dictatorship based on terror. His dictatorial power increased during the war and in the period after it. When Stalin died, Khrushchev inherited his apparatus but not the personal power that had accompanied it. During his initial years he had to work with Stalinist cadres, with leaders who themselves were guilty of numberless crimes. He accumulated personal power rather slowly, and altered the structure of the leadership. It took Brezhnev even longer to consolidate his personal position.

As a politician Andropov is closely linked with both the Khrushchev and the Brezhnev periods. He too must certainly want the freedom of action which will help him to make an impact on Soviet history. But in the conservative and corrupt political environment which he has inherited from Brezhnev, this may not be easy, even if he has no desire to introduce liberal reforms. Andropov needs new men, primarily able technocrats, simply to make the Soviet system more efficient. But even personnel changes are not straightforward and must obtain the approval of the Politburo, the Secretariat and the Central Committee. In Western democracies a change of leader usually means the transfer of power from one party to another. A new head of government can replace the entire administration and introduce a radically different social, economic and political programme. The limitations on a new leader in the Soviet Union are, in the first instance, more severe, since there are no constitutional guarantees that he will remain in power for a certain time. If Andropov's actions were to provoke serious objections amongst members of the Politburo and the Central Committee he could be replaced very quickly. This means that the initial period in office of a new leader in the Soviet Union is not as revealing as it might be in a Western democracy. One is forced to judge on the basis of very minor clues indeed. Some dissidents have been arrested or harassed. Does this mean a possible increase in repression? In January 1983 the first issue of the Party theoretical journal *Kommunist* mentioned Khrushchev's name three times in a positive context. This was immediately welcomed as an important liberal sign, because it would not have happened under Brezhnev. Even in his own memoirs about the virgin land programme, Brezhnev did not mention Khrushchev, despite the fact that all adult Soviet citizens know that he was the architect of this programme. From 1965 to 1981 Khrushchev's name was never mentioned in *Pravda* or in other central newspapers, apart from a three-line notice of his death, printed two days after it had occurred. Does the fact that his name has been mentioned in *Kommunist* represent a change of policy? One can only guess. Signs like these are never treated as accidental in Moscow.

The anti-corruption drive was welcomed by the general public, but it directly affects too many influential, highly placed officials. Almost all high officials enjoy privileges and benefits which they would be most reluctant to lose. Andropov's policy has come up against strong resistance, and there are recent signs that the intensity of the anti-corruption campaign has been significantly toned down. A corrupt chairman of a collective farm or a corrupt director of a factory can be exposed, but not a corrupt Minister or obkom secretary. There are signs that the cult of Brezhnev is slowly being dismantled. There are fewer of his numerous books on sale, his portraits are not being reprinted, and his name is rarely mentioned in Soviet papers. But this does not necessarily signal the end of the Brezhnev era, which can be defined as the rule of a conservative bureaucracy. Changes are inevitable simply through natural wastage. The younger technocratic generation will start to play a more important role in the next two or three years. Only then, when Brezhnev's old 'Dnepropetrovsk mafia' leaves the stage and is replaced

by men of Andropov's own choosing, will the Soviet Union
and the world at large find out what the Andropov succession really means.

It is difficult to make predictions about the main priorities
of the future Andropov era. He is undoubtedly a very clever
and ambitious man. But in his past political life his objectives
were usually rather narrow ones, and he appears to lack the
broad vision of a really popular leader. His few speeches and
papers hardly reveal his genuine political philosophy, since
in the Soviet Union this remains the privilege of the man of
the top – or of the dissidents. Andropov has waited for
supreme power for too long: if he wants to make his mark
on history, he must move faster than his predecessors. The
initial signs of his rule have been contradictory, but in the
realm of foreign policy he has contributed to the cause of
world peace. If he manages to achieve progress in nuclear
disarmament this would be the first time that the most
dangerous trend of post-war international development has
been reversed. But a clever political leader should try to
satisfy the main expectations of his people. For those in the
Soviet Union who think beyond immediate consumer satisfac-
tion, the main desire is, of course, to have more civil rights
and at least a moderate level of political democracy. There
are no signs yet that Andropov's domestic policy is making
even the slightest turn in this direction. I hope that time will
prove me wrong.

Notes and References

1 The Beginning of the Power Struggle

1 *The Sunday Times*, 15 January 1978.
2 *The Guardian*, 5 June 1979.
3 Zh. A. Medvedev, 'Russia under Brezhnev', *New Left Review*, No. 117, September 1979, p. 28.
4 *Time*, 15 March 1982, p. 15.
5 *Time*, 12 April 1982, p. 30.
6 *Newsweek*, 12 April 1982, p. 11.
7 *Newsweek*, 28 June 1982, p. 26.

2 Andropov as 'Chief Ideologue'

1 Boris Rabbot, 'Detente. The Struggle within the Kremlin', *Washington Post*, 10 July 1977, and 'A Letter to Brezhnev', *New York Times Magazine*, 6 November 1977.

3 General Secretary of the Central Committee

1 *Pravda*, 13 November 1982.
2 Ibid.

4 Andropov before 1957

1 *Pravda*, 13 November 1982 and other newspapers for the same date.
2 See English edition, 1973, vol. 2, p. 57.

3 *Pravda*, 13 November 1982.

4 *Smena*, No. 23–4, 1942.

5 *Komsomol'skaya Pravda*, 13 June 1943.

6 'Partiinyi kontrol' proizvoditel' nosti truda v promyshlen-nosti' (On Party control of the productivity of labour in industry), *Pravda*, 12 April 1951.

7 Joseph Kraft, 'Letter from Moscow', *The New Yorker*, 31 January 1983, p. 104.

8 Amongst Kraft's many distortions and errors was the statement that Roy wrote *Let History Judge* in collaboration with his twin brother, Zhores. In fact, he wrote it alone and it was published in English by Macmillan and A. Knopf in 1971.

9 Roy Medvedev, *Khrushchev*, London and New York: Blackwell and Doubleday, 1982, p. 58.

10 John Barron, *KGB*, New York: Reader's Digest Press, 1974, p. 72.

11 See, for example, the *Times* Diary of 13 November 1982. The *Times* version even adds that 'Maléter and his colleagues were shot that night'.

12 Bill Lomax, *Hungary 1956*, London: Allison and Busby, 1976; 'Andropov in Hungary', *L'Alternative* (forthcoming); and 'Andropov in Hungary', *The Times Higher Educational Supplement*, 10 December 1982; Béla Király, 'From Death to Revolution', *Dissent*, November–December 1966.

13 Lomax, 'Andropov in Hungary, *The Times Higher Educational Supplement*, 10 December 1982.

14 Kiraly, *op. cit.*, p. 727.

15 The story of Andropov's heart attack was reported by Dev Murarka in the *New Statesman*, 19 November 1982. There is no other confirmation of this.

16 *Khrushchev Remembers*, New York: Little Brown; London: André Deutsch, 1971, pp. 378–92.

5 Andropov as a Central Committee Secretary

1 Published much later in New York as *The Rise and Fall of T. D. Lysenko*, New York: Columbia University Press, 1969.

2 *Pravda*, 23 April 1964.

3 Yu. V. Andropov, *Izbrannye rechi i stat'yi*, Moscow: Politizdat, 1979, pp. 57–71.

4 Nineteen issues from various years were later published in Russian as Roy Medvedev (ed.), *Politicheskii Dnevnik*, Amsterdam: Herzen Foundation, 1975. Some materials from published and unpublished issues were translated and published in the USA in 1982 as S. F. Cohen (ed.), *An End to Silence. Uncensored opinion in the Soviet Union. From Roy Medvedev's underground magazine, 'Political Diary'*. Many of the unpublished issues have been deposited in the Slavic collections of the Firestone Library at Princeton University. Much of the material in this section relies upon this source.

5 See, for example, the articles by Marshall I. Bagramyan in *Literaturnaya gazeta*, 17 April 1965, by Troyanovsky in *Sovetskaya Rossiya*, 20 April 1965, and by Marshal I. Konev in *Pravda*, 19 April 1965.

6 *Problems of Peace and Socialism*, October 1964.

7 A. I. Solzhenitsyn, *The Oak and the Calf*, London: Collins and Harvil Press, 1980, p. 102.

8 Karyakin's case is described in Roy Medvedev (ed.), *Politicheskii Dnevnik*, vol. 2, Amsterdam: Herzen Foundation, 1975, p. 372. The text of Karyakin's speech has not been published but is available in *Political Diary*, No. 47, August 1968, in the Princeton University Library Russian collection.

9 Solzhenitsyn, *The Oak and the Calf*, pp. 98–9. Solzhenitsyn's sources of information about the power struggles were the same as Roy Medvedev's sources and mine – the editorial board of the liberal magazine *Novy Mir* and its editor, A. T. Tvardovsky, who was a member of the Central Committee. Yuri Karyakin, whose own position was in danger, had friends in the Party apparatus, and he too provided some details.

10 See *The Observer*, 2 December 1979.

11 There were no officially published comments on this conference. Information about it was reported in Roy Medvedev (ed.), *Politicheskii Dnevnik*, vol. 1, 1972, pp. 121–7.

6 Andropov becomes Head of the KGB

1 *Political Diary*, No. 33, June 1967.

7 The KGB under Andropov

1 John Barron, *KGB*, New York: Reader's Digest Press, 1974; Brian Freemantle, *KGB*, London: Michael Joseph/Rainbird, 1982.
2 Details about the changes in Azerbaijan can be found in *Political Diary*, No. 59, August 1969. In addition, many details were published in I. Zemzov, *Partiya ili Mafia* (*Party or Mafia*), Paris: Les Éditeurs Réunis, 1976. Zemzev, who emigrated in 1974, worked as a sociologist in Azerbaijan.
3 See *Politicheskii Dnevnik*, vol. 1, 1972, pp. 744–5.
4 These descriptions are all taken from *Newsweek* and *Time*, 22 November 1982. But similar comments were found in the *Washington Post, The Times, The New York Times, The Guardian, Die Zeit,* and *Der Spiegel.*
5 *The Sun, The Daily Mail.*
6 *The Observer*, 12 December 1982.

8 The KGB against Dissent

1 The Penal Code of the RSFSR, Moscow, 1963, 1964, and subsequent editions. The same article is included in the Penal (Criminal) Codes of the Ukraine, Georgia and other Republics. There is no common Penal Code for the whole of the USSR because the historical attitudes towards certain crimes vary in the different national Republics.
2 These speeches were widely circulating in *samizdat* and were later included in the book by L. Labedz and M. Hayward, *On Trial, the case of Sinyavsky (Tertz) and Daniel (Arzhak)*, London: Collins and Harvill Press, 1967.
3 Russian edition published, Amsterdam: Herzen Foundation, 1968; English translation published New York: Harper & Row, 1970.
4 The journal was mostly in *samizdat* until 1973, when it began to be published by Khronika Press, New York. The first *samizdat* issues were translated and classified in P. Reddaway's book *Uncensored Russia*, New York: American Heritage, 1972.

5 *Izvestiya*, 7 May 1977.
6 *The Sunday Times*, 14 November 1982.
7 Brezhnev's speech to the 26th Congress of Soviet Trade Unions, March 1977.
8 Published in all central Moscow newspapers on 10 September 1977.
9 *Izvestiya*, 10 September 1977.
10 Ibid.
11 P. G. Grigorenko, *Memoirs*, translated by T. Witney, New York and London: W. W. Norton, 1982, pp. 348–49.
12 *International Herald Tribune*, 9 December 1982.

9 The KGB against Brezhnev

1 Robert Daniels, 'The Two Faces of Brezhnev', *The New Leader*, 29 November 1982, p. 7.
2 *New York Post*, 5 November 1978.
3 See Konstantin M. Simis, *USSR: secrets of a corrupt society*, London: Dent, 1982.
4 *Pravda*, 24 August 1982.

10 Marshal Ustinov and the Military support Andropov

1 Leonid I. Brezhnev, *Pages from his Life*, written under the auspices of the Academy of Sciences of the USSR, New York: Simon and Schuster, 1978, p. 52.
2 Grigorenko, *Memoirs*, p. 183.
3 *Time*, 22 November 1982, pp. 25–6.
4 *Newsweek*, 12 April 1982, p. 11.

11 The New Man at the Top

1 *Wall Street Journal*, 12 November 1982.
2 Ibid.
3 Yu. V. Andropov, *Izbrannye rechi i stat'yi*, Moscow: Politizdat, 1979.

12 Forming a Team

1 See *International Herald Tribune*, 30 November 1982.
2 See, for example, Roy Medvedev, 'Changing of the Guard', *Baltimore Sun*, 25 June 1982, 'USSR after Brezhnev', *Marxism Today*, September 1982, pp. 18–25.
3 Medvedev, 'Changing of the Guard'.
4 Ibid.

13 Andropov's Economic Programme

1 *Newsweek*, 6 December 1982, p. 10.
2 *Izvestiya*, 17 December 1982.
3 See, for example, V. Romanuk, ('How prices are formed in the co-operative trade'), *Izvestiya*, 13 January 1983; M. Zarayev, ('Komissionnyi kilogram. How prices are set on meat in the co-operative trade'), *Sel'skaya zhizn'*, 14 January 1983, and many other similar articles.

14 The Drive against Corruption

1 See, for example, *Newsweek*, 18 April 1980, p. 22; *The Observer*, 27 July 1980.
2 See *Jews in the USSR*, Weekly Bulletin, London, vol. XI, No. 11, 11 March 1982, p. 2.
3 *Pravda*, 11 December 1982.

15 Changes in Domestic Policies

1 See, for example, Hélène Carrère d'Encausse, *Decline of an Empire. The Soviet Republics in Revolt*, New York: Newsweek Books, 1979.
2 See *Newsweek*, 29 December 1982, pp. 12–15.
3 *Newsweek*, 13 December 1982, p. 7.
4 For a full list of the categories, see the published decree in *Pravda*, 28 December 1982.

5 *Novy Mir*, Nos. 7, 8, 9, (1969). An English translation is forthcoming in autumn 1983, published by Quartet.
6 London: Jonathan Cape, 1979.
7 Dusko Doder, 'Soviet Official Gives Medvedev Formal Warning', *Washington Post*, 20 January 1983.
8 *Izvestiya*, 18 January 1983.

16 New Trends in Foreign Policy

1 Fyodor Burlatskii, 'Mezhdutsarstviye ili khronika vremyon
Den Syaopina' ('The interregnum or a chronicle of the times
of Den Sao Pin'), *Novy Mir*, April 1982, pp. 205–28.
2 Published in all central newspapers on 26 November 1982.
3 See *Vedomosti Verkhovnogo Soveta*, No. 34/1018, 30 August
1960.
4 See *Time*, 22 November 1982, pp. 25–6.
5 There are several good accounts of the events which led to
the 'April Revolution'. See, for example: Louis Duprée,
'Afghanistan under the Khalq', *Problems of Communism*,
Washington, July–August 1979; Selig Harrison, 'The Shah,
not Kremlin, Touched Off Afghan Coup', *Washington Post*,
13 May 1979; Fred Halliday, 'Revolution in Afghanistan',
New Left Review, No. 112, 1978, pp. 3–44, 'War and
Revolution in Afghanistan', *New Left Review*, No. 119,
1980, pp. 20–41.
6 N. I. Vavilov, *Izbrannye Trudy. Zemledelcheskii Afghanistan*
(*Selected Works: Agricultural Afghanistan*), vol. 1, Academy
of Sciences, USSR.
7 Press conference by Mr Peter Cutting, Chief Customs
Investigator, reported in *The Guardian* and *The Daily Telegraph*, 6 January 1983.
8 *Newsweek*, 22 November 1982, p. 23.
9 Ibid., p. 19.
10 Roy Medvedev, *Politicheskii Dnevnik*, Amsterdam: Herzen
Foundation, 1972, pp. 246–7.
11 *Time*, 27 December 1982, p. 16.
12 *Newsweek*, 29 November 1982, p. 15.
13 *Newsweek*, 22 November 1982, p. 19.

14 Zh. A. Medvedev, 'A break with the Brezhnev era', *Labour Weekly*, 19 November 1982, 'Yuri Andropov and his ways', *Labour Focus on Eastern Europe*, vol. 5, No. 5–6, 1982, pp. 2–6.

15 *International Herald Tribune*, 1–2 January 1983.

16 See B. Gwertzman, 'New CIA study shows Soviet Economic Gains', *International Herald Tribune*, 27 December 1982. The report was discussed in many other newspapers at the beginning of 1983.

17 *The Guardian*, 10 January 1983.

18 *Pravda, Izvestiya*, 7 January 1983.

19 *Pravda*, 22 December 1982.

20 Published by TASS on 5 January and in Soviet newspapers on 7 January 1983.

21 *The Guardian*, 8 January 1983.

22 *The Sunday Telegraph*, 9 January 1983.

23 TASS, 25 November 1982.

24 *Science*, vol. 218, 1982, p. 1100.

25 *The Guardian*, 14 January 1983.

Appendix
The Soviet Political System

The Party

The current system of Soviet leadership was established at the *Twenty-Sixth Congress* of the Communist Party of the Soviet Union, held in March 1981.

Congresses are convened every five years to discuss the Report of the Central Committee, the new five-year plan for economic development, and changes in the Party rules and programme.

The Congress also elects the new Party organs. So the Twenty-Sixth Congress elected a *Central Committee* of the CPSU consisting of 319 members and 151 candidate (alternative) members. The Central Committee meets in plenary session every 3–4 months. The Congress also elected a *Central Revision Commission* consisting of 75 members.

The Central Committee in its turn elected the *Politburo,* consisting of 14 members and 8 candidate members (see below), the *General Secretary* (L. I. Brezhnev, replaced by Yu. V. Andropov from 12 November 1982), the *Secretariat,* consisting of 10 members (see below), and the *Committee of Party Control,* whose Chairman is A. Ya. Pel'she.

The General Secretary usually chairs both the weekly meetings of the Politburo and the weekly (or if necessary, more frequent) meetings of the Secretariat. Each Secretary of the Central Committee presides over a group of related departments and sections of the Central Committee's permanent apparatus.

The apparatus of the Central Committee consists of about 25–6 different Departments (*otdely*), such as

Agriculture	Culture
Chemical Industry	Defence Industry

Foreign (socialist countries)	Party administration
Foreign (all other countries)	Propaganda and Agitation
General	Science and Education
Heavy Industry	Transport and
Light and Food Industry	Communication

The Central Committee apparatus also includes sections which work outside the larger departments as well as some research Institutes (e.g. the Institute of Marxism–Leninism, the Institute of the International Workers' Movements) and educational establishments (e.g. the Academy of Social Sciences, the Higher Party School). There are also some sections which deal with problems of a classified nature, such as censorship, permission for travel abroad for all Soviet citizens, etc.

The Supreme Soviet

The Supreme Soviet is the Soviet version of a bicameral Parliament. It is elected every 4 years and the two chambers, the *Council of the Union* and the *Council of Nationalities*, have equal powers and usually sit in joint session.

The Council of the Union is composed of deputies from about 900 constituencies (300,000 inhabitants in each).

The Council of Nationalities is composed of deputies elected on the basis of equal representation of every constituent republic – 32 deputies from each Union republic, 11 deputies from each autonomous republic, 5 deputies from each autonomous national region and 1 from each national okrug.

The Supreme Soviet is, as a rule, convened for regular sessions twice a year and works for two or three days during each session.

At the beginning of each four-year term the Supreme Soviet elects the *Presidium*, the *Chairman* and *Vice-Chairman* of the Presidium, and the *Council of Ministers*. These elections are carried out on the basis of official recommendations from the Central Committee of the Party. The General Secretary normally proposes a candidate for the post of Chairman of the Council of Ministers and the newly elected Premier proposes a list of Ministers.

PRESIDIUM OF THE SUPREME SOVIET	COUNCIL OF MINISTERS
Chairman (member of the Politburo)	Chairman (member of the Politburo)
First Vice-Chairman (candidate member of the Politburo)	3–4 First Vice-Chairmen
	12–13 Deputy Chairmen
	66 Ministers
15 Deputy Chairmen, one from every constituent Soviet republic	14 Chairmen of State Committees with ministerial status
23 members (some of them also members of the Politburo or Central Committee)	8 Chairmen of State Committees without ministerial status

The Presidium of the Supreme Soviet has full legislative power in the periods between sessions of the Supreme Soviet. It can dismiss and appoint ministers and ambassadors, pass new laws and appoint members of the Supreme Court. It works in collaboration with the 'Permanent Commissions of the Supreme Soviet' (on foreign affairs, education, environment, among others) which prepare draft proposals of new legislation.

At the brief full sessions of the Supreme Soviet, the annual budget, the annual economic plan and also the five-year plans become law. The Supreme Soviet can amend the constitution. It routinely confirms the laws and appointments which have already been made by the Presidium of the Supreme Soviet between sessions of the Supreme Soviet. All decisions are made by an open show of hands. There are no secret ballots.

The interlocking of the Party and government systems

The Heads of the Departments of the Central Committee are normally appointed by the Secretariat (and confirmed by the Politburo). Each department is divided into sections and subsections which in general correspond to the government ministries and departments. Thus the pattern of departments and sections changes when government structures change. The Department of Agriculture, for example, supervises the work of the Ministry of Agriculture, while related ministries (Tractors and Agricultural Machinery, Procurement, etc.) are supervised by parallel sections within the Department of Agriculture. Each branch of industry and every major professional field (higher education, middle education, sport, health service, publishing, etc.) is represented in the Central Committee apparatus either by a department or a section of a department. All major appointments (e.g. in the Academy of Sciences, or the Writers' Union, to editorial boards of professional journals, general magazines and newspapers, within ministries or in the diplomatic service) must be approved by the appropriate departments and sections of the Central Committee. All the positions which require this approval are usually considered to be *nomenklatura* positions.

The same rules apply to the structure of the Republican Party Congresses and Central Committees and the government bodies at that level.

The interlocking of the Party and the government apparatus is based on traditional, unwritten rules which are not made explicit in the constitution. The Chairman of the Supreme Soviet and the Premier must be members of the Politburo. Some key ministers (e.g. Defence, and Foreign Affairs at present) are also members of the Politburo. Most other ministers and chairmen of State Committees are either members or candidate members of the Central Committee or Central Revision Commission. The level of seniority in the Party of ministers and chairmen of State Committees usually reflects the importance of their organizations in national affairs. The chairmen of the Permanent Commissions of the Supreme Soviet are usually the heads of the related departments or sections of the Central Committee. Members of the Central Committee usually serve as deputies of the Supreme Soviet elected from different constituencies.

Important decisions on current economic and political problems are usually introduced as joint resolutions of the Central Committee and Council of Ministers. Between plenary sessions of the Central Committee, joint decisions of the Politburo and Secretariat are usually presented as decisions of the Central Committee. Between full meetings of the Council of Ministers, decisions of the Presidium of the Council of Ministers (Chairman, First Vice-

Chairmen and Deputy Chairmen) are presented as decisions of the Council of Ministers.

Regional Party secretaries are normally elected as members or candidate members of the Central Committee and as deputies of the Supreme Soviet from one of the constituencies in their region.

In the Soviet decision-making process the Party system (via the Politburo or Central Committee) gives *directives*. The Supreme Soviet (via the Presidium) formulates them as *laws* and *appointments* and the Council of Ministers implements them as *practical measures*. Internal Party appointments and problems are dealt with by the Secretariat.

The Politburo and Secretariat as elected at the Twenty-Sixth Party Congress, 1981

POLITBURO	CENTRAL COMMITTEE SECRETARIAT
Members	
L. I. Brezhnev (also Chairman of Presidium of Supreme Soviet)	General Secretary
Yu. V. Andropov (also Chairman of KGB)	
K. U. Chernenko	Secretary in charge of General Department
M. S. Gorbachev	Secretary dealing with agriculture
V. V. Grishin (also First Secretary of Moscow obkom)	
A. A. Gromyko (also Minister of Foreign Affairs)	
A. P. Kirilenko	Secretary dealing with organizational matters
D. A. Kunaev (also First Secretary of Kazakhstan Communist Party)	
A. Ya. Pel'she (also Chairman of the Committee of Party Control)	

G. V. Romanov (also First
Secretary of Leningrad obkom)

V. V. Shcherbitsky (also First
Secretary of Ukraine
Communist Party)

M. A. Suslov   Secretary dealing with ideology

N. A. Tikhonov (also Chairman
of Council of Ministers of   † V. I. Dolgikh: industry
USSR)
                                                † I. V. Kapitonov: in charge of
D. F. Ustinov (also Minister of   Party organizational work
Defence)
                                                † K. V. Rusakov: in charge of
Candidate Members   foreign department (socialist
* G. A. Aliyev (also First   countries)
Secretary of Azerbaijan
Communist Party)   † M. V. Zimyanin: assistant to
                                                Brezhnev and foreign affairs
P. N. Demichev (also Minister
of Culture)

T. Ya. Kiselyev (also First
Secretary of Byelorussian
Communist Party)

V. V. Kuznetsov (also Deputy
Chairman of Presidium of
Supreme Soviet)

B. N. Ponomarev   Secretary in charge of foreign
                                                department (non-socialist
                                                countries)

Sh. R. Rashidov (also First
Secretary of Uzbekistan
Communist Party)

E. A. Shevarnadze (also First
Secretary of Georgian
Communist Party)

M. S. Solomentsev (also
Chairman of Council of
Ministers of RSFSR)

   * Promoted to full membership November 1982
   † Central Committee Secretary but not member of Politburo

Glossary

apparatchik	familiar term for an official in the Party 'apparatus', e.g. the head of a section or a department
cadre	a paid Party official. Members of the various Party committees are either professional workers, who receive a salary, or elected representatives, who retain their usual jobs while serving
CPSU	Communist Party of the Soviet Union
Cheka	the name by which the secret police – members of the Extraordinary Commission for Struggle with Counter-Revolution and Sabotage – were known before that organization was disbanded in 1922
dacha	holiday house, usually in the country or at a resort. For officials it usually means a special, state-owned villa, given either for a certain period or for life
General Procurator	combines the function of public prosecutor and investigator as well as supervision of prisons and of the legal system. Appointed by the Supreme Soviet. There are local pro-curators subordinated to the Procurator-General in Moscow
Gosplan	the state planning committee

Gulag

abbreviation of *Glavnoye upravleniye lagerei* (Department of Camp Administration, within the KGB and MVD). The abbreviation is unofficial slang used by the prisoners and popularized by Alexander Solzhenitsyn

KGB

abbreviation of *Komitet gosudarstvennoi bezopasnosti* (Committee of State Security)

kolkhozes, *kolkhozniks*

collective farms, members of collective farms

Komsomol

abbreviation of *Kommunisticheskii soyuz molodezhi* (Young Communist League), the mass movement to which the majority of young people belong

MGB

abbreviation of *Ministerstvo gosudarstvennoi bezonasnosti* (Ministry of State Security), which existed from 1946 to 1953

MVD

abbreviation of *Ministerstvo vnutrennikh del* (Ministry of Internal Affairs)

NKVD

abbreviation of *Narodnyi kommissariat vnutrennikh del* (People's Commissariat of Internal Affairs). Until 1946 all Ministries were called People's Commissariats

nomenklatura

the list of important tenured positions in the Party and state apparatus, appointment to which requires approval from higher Party bodies. Originally from *nomenklaturnyi rabotnik*, which meant a professional official of the Party and state apparatus. Some people are elected to important committees for a single term only, in order to demonstrate popular democracy. Others on the *nomenklatura* are Party or state professionals who are to be re-elected or promoted to similar or higher positions in other parts of the country

obkom   abbreviation of *oblastnoi komitet* (regional Party committee)

OVIR   the department of visas and registrations of the MVD. There are no official emigration or immigration services in the USSR, but the job of arranging emigration is performed by OVIR, which also arranges private foreign trips

Party–State Control Committee   set up by Khrushchev in 1962 as a powerful joint organ of control attached to both the Central Committee and the Council of Ministers. It was abolished after Khrushchev fell from power and replaced by a committee of lower status, the People's Control Committee

Politburo   the political bureau of the Central Committee of the CPSU. The top decision-making body in the Soviet political system. It was called the Presidium between 1952 and 1966. Members are either full members, with voting rights, or candidate members, who attend proceedings but cannot vote

Pravda   the newspaper organ of the Central Committee of the CPSU

samizdat   works of literature, politics, etc. reproduced by copying, photocopying, or typing, and distributed by individuals outside the official censorship system

Supreme Soviet   Soviet parliament consisting of elected deputies in two houses, one based on nationalities, the other on demographic electoral constituencies. Only one candidate – usually proposed by the local Party organization – stands for each seat. Deputies work as legislators only during sessions of the Supreme Soviet, which last two or three days each and take place twice a year. The Supreme Soviet tends to function as a rubber-stamping organization approving laws already passed by the Presidium of the Supreme Soviet

Union republics   the Soviet Union is made up of fifteen republics which are called Union republics (or constituent or national republics). Where there are large and distinct national minorities, Union republics may be further subdivided into autonomous republics and autonomous regions

Index